# Drew Brees: The Inspiring Story of One of Football's Most Resilient Quarterbacks

An Unauthorized Biography

By: Clayton Geoffreys

# Table of Contents

# Foreword

Drew Brees has had a storied career as quarterback of the New Orleans Saints. Brees' football legacy really began at Purdue University, where he was one of the most celebrated quarterbacks in school and conference history. Since that time, Brees has won the Super Bowl once, while also being selected to multiple Pro Bowl teams as a member of the New Orleans Saints. There is a reason why Brees was the NFL's Comeback Player of the Year in 2004: he has a huge heart when it comes to playing the game of football. And you'll discover this in this unauthorized biography. In this updated edition, I've reworked the original manuscript to listen to what past readers have shared they wished I had covered more, and added more in-depth coverage of some of the latest seasons of Drew Brees' career. Thank you for purchasing *Drew Brees: The Inspiring Story of One of Football's Most Resilient Quarterbacks*. In this unauthorized biography, we will learn Drew Brees' incredible life story and impact on the game of football. Hope you enjoy and if you do, please do not forget to leave a review!

Also, check out my website at claytongeoffreys.com to join my exclusive list where I let you know about my latest books. To thank you for your purchase, you can go to my site to download a free copy of *33 Life Lessons: Success Principles, Career Advice & Habits of Successful People*. In the book, you'll learn from some of the greatest thought leaders of different industries on what it takes to become successful and how to live a great life. I'll also include some other sports biographies for you to read!

Cheers,

*Clayton Geoffreys*

*Visit me at www.claytongeoffreys.com*

# Introduction

Many people recognize Drew Christopher Brees as the successful quarterback of the New Orleans Saints. He has a great career, a beautiful family, several lucrative endorsement deals, and a Super Bowl championship ring. He has it made.

Or does he?

A lot of individuals do not realize that Brees has gone through all sorts of adversity–injuries, his parents' divorce, and his mother's suicide, among other things–to get where he is today. He relied on his faith and persistence to reach new heights.

Just like you and me, Brees has had to deal with doubts. His childhood dream was to be a professional baseball player. Along the way, he changed course and decided to pursue a football career instead. It was not going to be an easy path, either. He suffered an injury in high school which made him think that his gridiron dream was in jeopardy. What made him stay the course? Why did he persevere through it all?

Brees' life has had several interesting twists and turns. For instance, he thought he would spend his entire career with the San Diego Chargers, the team that drafted him 32nd overall in 2001. Alas, an unfortunate incident led him to sign with the

New Orleans Saints instead. Brees' career was not always rosy. Even if he helped the Saints win the Vince Lombardi Trophy in the 2009 NFL season, he also endured many losing campaigns. He may be a superstar athlete, but he has had ups and downs just like everyone else. His story inspires us to be the best version of ourselves we can be no matter what life throws our way.

# Chapter 1: Early Life and Childhood Years

Drew Christopher Brees was born on January 15, 1979, in Austin, Texas to parents who were both lawyers. His father is named Eugene Brees and is often called "Chip" by his friends and peers alike. Drew's mother is named Mina Ruth.

*Sports Illustrated*'s Tim Layden wrote a piece about Drew Brees on August 16, 1999. In it, he said that Chip and Mina Brees named their son after Drew Pearson, the former Dallas Cowboys wide receiver-turned-sportscaster. Drew Brees refuted this in December 2014 and said that there was no truth to that legend.[i]

Nature also set the younger Brees apart from everyone else on the day he was born. He sported a prominent birthmark on his right cheek.

Layden described the birthmark as approximately "the size, shape, and texture of a small woolly-bear caterpillar." He then wrote that Chip Brees "recoiled at the sight of the brown patch." From her perspective, Mina Brees thought that a previous slip on an icy footpath might have caused the birthmark. Years later, she would tell her son that the birthmark was caused by "an angel's kiss."[ii] Chip and Mina Brees thought about removing the birthmark surgically. However, they eventually changed their minds.[iii]

Drew Brees wrote an autobiography entitled *Coming Back Stronger: Unleashing the Hidden Power of Adversity* in 2010. He never saw it as a bad thing and started looking at it as something that made him unique and special compared to other people. He valued being someone different physically instead of risking the chance that it might cause health problems.[iv]

In hindsight, Brees said it probably would have been better to remove the birthmark. Taking a chance on something that may have been cancerous was risky. He revealed that he had the birthmark biopsied as an adult and that he also occasionally visits his dermatologist to make sure it does not pose a health threat.

Despite Brees' birthmark being benign, it still gave him trouble in a different way.

In his 2010 book, he said that his childhood was not easy. Many kids at his school taunted him because of the prominent birthmark.

"They used to tease me and take jabs at me in the classroom and on the playground, saying things like, 'What happened to your face?' or, 'Wipe that stuff off your face.'"

Brees admitted that he got into a few fights in school because of it.

When his autobiography came out in 2010, he was 31 years old. He said that the birthmark is "just a part of who I am." He emphasized that he would never cut his arm off. That being the case, he would not remove his birthmark, either. He said that his long-time friends do not even notice it anymore when they were hanging out. Instead, they just saw him for who he is.

When Drew Brees was already an established superstar quarterback in the National Football League (NFL), he realized that the birthmark was a blessing because it helped toughen him up. To his credit, he saw it as something that helped him build his character because of how it allowed him to shake off any kind of criticism. It made him tough inside and he was able to shut off jabs and off-hand comments.

He turned out to be right in a lot of ways.

Brees honed his work ethic during his childhood years in Texas. The future quarterback practiced his throwing accuracy by flinging rocks at any object he saw in the family's backyard. He would do this over and over. His younger brother Reid (who is nearly three years younger) and their friends would join in on the fun. The brothers' age gap served as a huge physical advantage for Drew back then. He would kneel down whenever they played football to give his younger brother a fair chance.

In his book, Drew Brees described their playground as a small space that was no bigger than most living rooms. That small patch of grass was where he played a lot of football when he was a child. There were a lot of trees that served as their sidelines whenever they played and they resorted to imaginary goal lines.

Chip Brees raved about Drew's competitive nature in a December 2000 interview with the Associated Press (via *The Lafayette Journal & Courier*).

"Drew always had a competitive streak," he said. "He always wanted to create a contest out of something. A lot of times, it was just trying to throw a rock and hit a telephone pole or trash can…He was always accurate, and he always had a good arm."[v]

He would sometimes join his children and their friends' games in their backyard.

Drew Brees said there were many pictures of him as a child holding either a football or baseball. It came as no surprise to anyone because he came from a family that had sports running in the bloodline.

His mother, Mina, was all-state in high school in three sports: track and field, volleyball, and basketball. Drew is proud of the fact that his mother was one of the first women who attended Texas A&M University, which was, at the time, an all-male military school.

It was Mina Brees who influenced her sons to take up tennis.

"I wanted both Drew and his brother to be great tennis players because that's my favorite sport," she told SportsLine (via GaleGroup.com) in 2000. "I hate to confess this, but I probably didn't encourage him enough to be a football player. I was hoping he could be the next Pete Sampras or Andre Agassi."[vi]

Her husband, Chip, suited up for Texas A&M's freshman basketball team. He met Mina when they were both in college.

Drew Brees' younger brother, Reid, was a member of the 2005 Baylor Bears baseball team which made it to the 2005 College World Series in Omaha, Nebraska. The Bears advanced to the second round where they lost to the Texas Longhorns, 4-3.

The Brees brothers had aspired to play in the College World Series since they were young boys. It was Drew's dream even before he became a football player. To have seen his brother live out their dream was "one of the proudest moments in my life," per his autobiography.

Athleticism also runs deep in Drew Brees' other family members.

His uncle on his mother's side of the family, Marty Atkins, was an All-American quarterback for the Texas Longhorns, the Texas A&M Aggies' fierce rivals. Atkins played for the Longhorns when Texas beat Paul "Bear" Bryant and the Alabama Crimson Tide in the 1973 Cotton Bowl.

Brees' grandfather, Ray Atkins, served in the Second Great War. After World War II, he coached at Gregory-Portland High School in Portland, Texas for 38 years. He won 302 games and became a household name in the state due to his accomplishments as a coach.

When Brees was around seven years old, he and his brother Reid would hand out water mixed with electrolytes to their grandfathers' players during timeouts. The older Brees was excited to be part of the action at such a young age.

His family's get-togethers also revolved around sports. Whether it was Thanksgiving Day, Christmas, Easter, or Independence Day, they would play games in the backyard after feasting on large meals. Drew Brees loved to play games when he was a child. Interestingly enough, the game did not need to have a ball for him to play it.

At this point in his life, Drew Brees toughened himself up in two ways: dealing with criticism for having a prominent birthmark and playing all sorts of games with his family and friends.

But the toughest part of his childhood was yet to come.

Brees said his parents divorced when he was around seven years old and his brother Reid was five years old. In his book, he stated that he recalled seeing his parents sitting down to talk things over. He had high hopes they would be able to reconcile their differences.

However, Chip Brees sat down with his two boys one day to tell them about the status of his marriage with Mina. When Drew Brees saw his father remove his glasses, he expected the worst—he only saw him take them off when Chip Brees cleaned them or when he became emotional. He knew his dad would resort to the latter action.

Chip Brees told his sons that he and his mother would go their separate ways. Drew Brees described it as a very painful moment—it still brings a tear to his eye to this very day. He described the split as hostile and bitter. They cried themselves to sleep for many nights after the painful divorce.

In the aftermath of the split, Drew and Reid Brees would divide their time between their father and mother. On some days, they would be with the former, and on other days of the week, they would be with the latter.

As children, their escape from this trying time was fishing. They brought their buckets and nets to a nearby creek to catch fish and crayfish. Other than fish, they also spent time trying to fish out golf balls. They sold the balls to golfers and made enough money to buy simple things such as baseball cards. Just the usual things that kids did.

Drew Brees believed his parents' divorce forged an inseparable bond between himself and his brother. They dealt with the tragedy together. They did not let anything stand between them, even at such a young age.

Drew would continue to excel in sports. He broke the Austin, Texas Little League home run record when he was 12 years old.

Not only that, but he also earned the number one ranking among tennis players in his age bracket that same year.

He attended St. Andrew's Episcopal School, a renowned private school, from sixth until the eighth grade. He cites his mother as the primary reason he wound up in the school. Mina Brees wanted her son to get substantial experience in both academics and athletics.

Chip Brees would not relent at first. He was hesitant to send his first-born son to a private school. Drew remembered his parents' choice of school was one of the topics they argued about frequently. Brees described his father as "easygoing" in his autobiography. On the other hand, he dubbed his mother as "overly competitive."

In the end, Mina Brees got her way. Drew finished his elementary school years at St. Andrew's.

# Chapter 2: High School Years

As Drew Brees entered high school, he started building a successful athletics career. However, it did not happen at St. Andrew's Episcopal School.

He transferred to Westlake High School by the time he reached ninth grade. Again, it was his mother who made the decision for him. Mina Brees felt that Westlake offered Drew not only good education but also a competitive athletic program that would help develop his love for sports.

Drew Brees described the situation in his book: "I remember some conflict between my mom and dad about the school decision," he said. "When she and dad would argue, she'd refuse to back down. Whenever she'd get in that bulldog mode, my dad would have no other choice than to agree with her decision."

Brees played flag football from the age of 12 until he reached the ninth grade and transferred from St. Andrew's. It was his parents' way of making sure that he was ready for the game's physical grind in the ensuing years, according to the Associated Press. It was there at St. Andrew's that he developed his most basic skills as a football player by working on the fundamentals of throwing, catching, and running–the same things that quarterbacks needed to master.

Unfortunately, the small Christian school did not have enough players for them to play tackle football. In a way, this was a good thing for Drew Brees because it allowed him to stay healthy and injury-free before reaching high school.

When Brees reported for his first taste of Texas 5A football at Westlake, he remembered seeing around 150 to 200 other kids at the tryout. The coach asked the group who wanted to play quarterback. Brees raised his hand. But so did 40 other players.

He felt that he had no chance. Nonetheless, he wound up fourth in the six-quarterback depth chart of the Westlake Chaparrals. He was merely the starter in the second team and had to play behind three other quarterbacks regarded as "better" than he was back then.

One day during his sophomore year at Westlake, his mother picked him up from school. When they pulled into the driveway, she knew something was amiss because her son seemed a lot more quiet than usual. Brees spoke up. He told his mother that he was thinking about quitting football. It was the first time he mentioned quitting.

When Mina Brees asked why, Drew told her he felt that he would not be able to improve as a football quarterback with the Westlake football team because of how he did not have a lot of opportunities to do so. Back then, Johnny Rodgers was the starting quarterback of the Westlake Chaparrals. Johnny's third brother was his teammate and starting center. Their other brother, also named Johnny, started at quarterback for the junior varsity squad. To top it all off, their father was the Texas Longhorns' recruiting coordinator. Brees thought his dream was in serious jeopardy.

He then told his mother that he might make the switch to baseball and get a scholarship. He and his brother Reid always dreamed about playing in the College World Series. They also collected baseball cards when their parents divorced several years earlier.

Mina Brees then said something which would make a profound impact on him. She told her son that he did had a valid point but that did not mean that he did not have the opportunity to rise up. It may have been bad for Mina to see her son on the bench but she made a point to Drew that opportunity will always present itself when it is needed.

To that end, Drew Brees then told his mother that he would continue playing in two-a-day football practices at Westlake and hope for the best. Mina Brees' words turned out to be prophetic the very next week.

Drew said that two junior quarterbacks dropped out of the offensive roster. The first one joined the baseball team while the other changed positions and wanted to play defense instead of offense. Now he was Westlake's second quarterback on the depth chart next to Johnny Rodgers.

Unfortunately for Rodgers, he tore his ACL when the Killeen Kangaroos sacked him in Westlake High School's last scrimmage game before the season. He would have to miss the entire season due to the injury.

Drew Brees was now the starting quarterback of Westlake's junior varsity team. He had made it from a field of 200 quarterback aspirants during football tryouts. He promptly guided the Chaparrals to a 10-0 record his sophomore year. The team also enjoyed an undefeated streak in his junior year as they were able to make it as far as the third round of the playoffs that season.

That was when Drew Brees stumbled on another obstacle: He also tore his ACL.

Just when Brees had finally made a name for himself as the Chaparrals' starting JV quarterback, he injured his knee in December 1995. Doctors declared that his season was over. Consequently, Westlake High lost in the next round.

At the time of the critical injury, Brees said he had been receiving recruiting letters from renowned football programs. When the injury happened, schools stopped sending him messages. The Texas A&M Aggies and Texas Longhorns already had starting quarterbacks in place. The Baylor Bears, TCU Horned Frogs, and Texas Tech Red Raiders all passed him up. Brees felt the Rice Owls' option offense was not a good fit for his skills. On the other hand, the SMU Mustangs were still reeling from the "death penalty" the NCAA had imposed on their program for providing under-the-table payments to their athletes in the 1970s and 1980s.

Brees, his dad Chip, and stepmother Amy even went to the University of North Carolina to visit then-head football coach Mack Brown. Brees liked the school very much. According to *The Chicago Tribune's* Andrew Bagnato, the Brees camp "presented a national highlight tape." Brown thanked them for their time.[vii]

Several months later, one of Brown's assistants told Brees he did not make the North Carolina Tar Heels' roster. Brees told Bagnato he understood why Brown did not consider him.

"I'm a skinny, runt-looking kid," he said. "I just had my knee surgery a couple of months before, and I'm hobbling around. I wouldn't have recruited me, either."

His mom Mina also reached out to several football programs hoping they would consider her son. She got through to big-name coaches such as the BYU Cougars' LaVell Edwards and the Iowa Hawkeyes' Hayden Fry. They both said that their quarterback rosters were full. Other head football coaches told her the same thing.

It seemed that Brees had no feasible options regarding reputable Division I football programs. Because of this, he thought about playing basketball or baseball as a backup plan. In fact, he was hoping he could earn a baseball scholarship. However, the prospects looked grim because of his injury.

Brees underwent surgery to repair the torn ACL. He then wore a knee brace and used crutches for six weeks. His doctors gave him a six-month timeline for his rehabilitation. After the six weeks were up, Brees put himself through rigorous three or four-hour training sessions at the school gym every day so the knee would recover faster.

He considered the injury as a crucial turning point in his life. He had to make the same decision he made two years earlier when he was at the bottom of the Westlake quarterback rotation: Would he quit or keep fighting?

During Brees' recovery, he went to church with his dad Chip at First Baptist Church in Austin, Texas. Drew admitted he was not into church all that much. He would usually nod off or scan the congregation for attractive girls.

On this day, he listened to a sermon from Dr. Browning Ware about God's plan for one's life. Dr. Ware cited the famous Tom Cruise movie from 1992, *A Few Good Men*. In Brees' words, Dr. Ware was "looking for a few good men to carry on his teachings and to walk the walk with Christ." At that moment, Brees realized the message resonated deeply with him–he wanted to be one of those few good men.

Brees was confused because he did not know for sure if he would ever play football again. At the same time, he felt a sense of peace he had never felt before. For the first time in his life, he knew that God was in control of his destiny.

"I couldn't escape the sense that God's plan for me was to come back stronger and lead my team again," he said in his 2010 autobiography.

Brees also realized he was not in the best physical shape of his life when he was injured. He stood six feet tall and weighed 170 pounds–not the typical build of a future star quarterback. It was then that he started working harder at the gym. Not only did he want to rehab his knee, but he also wanted to put on more muscle mass to help him become an outstanding quarterback.

Brees trained hard under the watchful eye of Carment Kiara, a high school football coach in Austin, Texas. Not only did Brees train in the weight room, but he also ran uphill in the oppressive Texas heat (something Texans refer to as "The Siege" because of how hot it can be). The coach was impressed with Brees and said that this young man was a doer and someone who never doubted himself one bit.

Brees' persistence paid off. He put on 25 pounds of muscle mass, and six months after he underwent surgery, he was ready to take the field once again. Along the way, he also renewed his courage and confidence, two things which he would lean on for the rest of his life.

Brees picked up where he left off. He led Westlake High to an undefeated 16-0 season in his senior year and led the Chaparrals to their first-ever 5A state football championship.

Several months earlier, Drew Brees felt that his entire world had crumbled. However, he decided to use the adversity that he faced to his advantage. As a result, he improved in all aspects: physically, mentally, and spiritually. Even if he had yet to receive new recruiting letters, he remained unfazed. He knew the best was yet to come.

Brees also did not make it to SuperPrep's Texas 102 after his senior season at Westlake High School. Tom Lemming also overlooked Brees in the All-Southwest Team in his annual Prep Football Report. Recruiters paid more attention to his lack of height and awkward running style than his accomplishments (which included a sterling 28-0-1 record when he started for Westlake).

However, it turned out that Brees did not have to wait very long for his next opportunity. Exactly a year after Brees blew out his knee, he caught the attention of a few college teams. Among these were the Kentucky Wildcats and the Purdue Boilermakers. Both programs had several similarities. They had new coaches– Hal Mumme called the shots for the Wildcats while Joe Tiller took charge for the Boilermakers. Both Kentucky and Purdue ran spread offenses, which meant a quarterback with a great arm was one of the centerpieces. The two programs had a month and a half to finish their recruitment, and the quarterback class was thinning out. Brees happened to be one of the few capable quarterbacks still available.

Ironically, the turn of events occurred just a week after Westlake Chaparrals offensive coordinator Neal LaHue had approached Brees and asked him if anybody had already recruited him. Brees replied in the negative. It just so happened that both the Wildcats' and Boilermakers' scouts showed up at the same Westlake High practice.

Even though the two schools were keen on Brees, he still set his sights on his lifelong dream of attaining a baseball scholarship. In his 2010 autobiography, he even mentioned that he had aspirations of playing in the majors someday.

Brees went on recruiting trips to Brown University, the University of Kentucky, and Purdue University. In the end, he decided to attend Purdue because of its academic reputation (in his book, he referred to it as "the Ivy League of the Midwest"). He also chose Purdue because of Coach Tiller and the spread offense he ran. Brees felt that it would be a perfect fit for him.

He was also excited to play in the Big Ten Conference. Even if Purdue was considered a basketball school, he thought nothing of it.

Several years later, he and his teammates would put Purdue football on the map.

Brees was part of a 15-player recruiting class that was dead last in the Big Ten, but that did not dissuade them one bit. Once they got together, they had one goal: to become Big Ten champions and win the Rose Bowl. They were out to prove the naysayers wrong.

Drew Christopher Brees finished his high school football career at Westlake High School as the Texas 5A Most Valuable Offensive Player in his senior year, 1996. He also amassed 5,461 passing yards and 51 touchdowns on a 64 percent completion rate.[viii] Brees and his good friend LaDainian Tomlinson (a TCU Horned Frogs alumnus and future running back great with the San Diego Chargers and the New York Jets) also made it to the 1997 *USA Today* All-USA High School Football Team.[ix] Brees certainly had come a long way from his flag football days and early struggles at Westlake.

Now he was about to take his talents and newfound confidence to West Lafayette, Indiana.

# Chapter 3: College Years at Purdue University

Drew Brees was about to make the transition from Texas 5A football with the Westlake High Chaparrals to Big Ten football with the Purdue Boilermakers. He was just as awestruck when he saw the Purdue University campus as he was when he visited the University of North Carolina several months earlier.

Brees described the end of the school week and the eve of Saturday game days as some of his best memories at Purdue. He majored in industrial engineering and was a member of the Sigma Chi Fraternity.

Brees had no regrets about playing for the Boilermakers. He was proud of the way head football coach Joe Tiller structured all of the teams Brees played for during his four-year stint.

He said that Tiller had two simple rules: Do what you are supposed to do, and follow the so-called "Golden Rule." In Brees' words, the latter one meant "he who has the gold makes all the rules." If a player broke either of these rules, he would work out at 6 a.m. or participate in the dreaded "throw-up session." Here, the rulebreaker would run, do up-downs, and barrel rolls to the point that they would vomit.

According to Purdue University's official athletics website, Brees did not make much of an impact in his freshman year. He suited up in just seven games as a backup to starter Billy Dicken. He recorded just 232 passing yards and 1 interception in his first year as a Big Ten quarterback. Brees had his best game of the year on September 6, 1997. He converted on 11 of 21 pass attempts for 97 yards against the Toledo Rockets. Purdue finished with a 9-3 win-loss record and went on to beat the Oklahoma State Cowboys in the 1997 Builders Square Alamo Bowl, 33-20.

This was not something new to Drew Brees. After all, he spent a lot of his time as a backup when he was still a young boy trying to learn how to play the quarterback position. But, as always, Drew Brees was relentless in his pursuit of an opportunity to show why he was worthy of a starting spot.

Brees did not start for the Boilermakers until his sophomore season in 1998. His first game as Purdue's starting quarterback was in the Pigskin Classic against the USC Trojans on August 30th. The Boilermakers held a 17-7 halftime lead but lost 27-17. Brees threw his first touchdown as a Big Ten quarterback when he passed to wide receiver Gabe Cox at the 10:20 mark of the first quarter. Brees converted 30 of 52 pass attempts for 248 yards and 2 touchdowns in a losing effort.[x]

Two weeks later, the Boilermakers played their first game before a crowd of 42,563 at Ross-Ade Stadium in West Lafayette, Indiana. Brees threw for 250 yards, 2 touchdowns, and ran for another one in the narrow 21-19 win on September 12th.[xi]

Brees looked forward to the fourth game of the season, a matchup against the in-state powerhouse, the Notre Dame Fighting Irish. The Boilermakers had never beaten the Irish in Notre Dame Stadium since 1973. Adding to the excitement, NBC was broadcasting the game to a national television audience. The country was about to get its first glimpse of the Austin, Texas native who played quarterback at Purdue University. At the time, Brees considered the Notre Dame contest as "the biggest game of my life."

Notre Dame was coming off a Bowl Championship Series game in 1997. The Irish also played very toughly on the defensive end, but Brees remained unfazed. He led Purdue to a 21-14 halftime lead. He went 17-of-21 passing for 2 touchdowns in the first 58 minutes of the game. With a 30-28 lead in the final 1:58, all Purdue needed to do was to run out the clock to secure the upset.

The Fighting Irish would not flinch.

They forced the Boilermakers to a key third-and-15 situation. Purdue's offensive coordinator, Jim Chaney, called for a pass play to wide receiver Randall Lane while Brees rolled out to his left. Unfortunately, the ball bounced off Lane's hands and landed right on Notre Dame free safety Tony Driver. Interception. Driver drove the length of the field all the way to Purdue's five-yard line. The Irish kicked a field goal to take the lead, 31-30.

Purdue still had a chance with less than a minute left in the game. On second down, Brees threw an interception similar to the one several plays earlier. Notre Dame took a knee and ran out the clock. The winning streak against the Boilermakers was intact.

Brees decided that he was not going to let one game ruin his entire season. He felt that he played well for the most part against Notre Dame. He just found it hard to shake off the sting of the two last-minute interceptions he had thrown. He wanted to put that in the past and play to the best of his abilities moving forward.

It did not take long for Brees to get over the Notre Dame loss. He threw for a school-record 522 yards and 6 touchdowns in the 56-21 win over the Minnesota Golden Gophers on October 3,

1998. Brees would throw for six touchdowns again in a win over the Northwestern Wildcats on November 7th. Ironically, the Boilermakers prevailed with the very same score, 56-21.

After the win over Minnesota, Purdue lost their next two games against the Wisconsin Badgers and the Penn State Nittany Lions.

Brees made it to the NCAA record books when he recorded 83 pass attempts in the 31-24 loss to the Badgers. The NCAA's official website confirms it is a single-game record for attempts. Brees converted on 55 of them—18 to wide receiver Randall Lane—for a total of 494 yards; he also threw 4 interceptions.

Brees' longest pass attempt was 21 yards. Lane finished with 178 receiving yards while the other Purdue wide receiver, Chris Daniels, recorded 131 receiving yards.

Following the game, Brees commented that he and his teammates had just taken what the Wisconsin defense gave them. "Eight-three might have been a little excessive," he said. "But that's what we felt we had to do to win. We're going to take what the defense gives us. The thing is, I could have thrown 100 that game. I felt great."[xii]

Wisconsin head football coach Barry Alvarez gushed at Brees' performance. "You couldn't hear yourself think, and he just couldn't be rattled," he told *The Chicago Tribune* (via NCAA.com). "He put on as impressive a performance as I've ever seen."[xiii]

The Boilermakers regrouped to win their next six games to finish the season 9-4. They won their second consecutive bowl game when they beat the favored Kansas State Panthers, 27-24, in the 1998 Alamo Bowl in San Antonio, Texas. Brees had a mediocre game with 22 for 50 passing for 175 yards, 2 touchdowns, and 3 interceptions.[xiv] Nonetheless, Brees performed when it mattered, orchestrating the game-winning touchdown drive in the final 30 seconds.

Drew Brees had arrived. The media named him the Big Ten Offensive Player of the Year. He set school and conference records with 569 pass attempts, 361 completions, 3,983 passing yards, and 39 touchdowns. He also completed 63.4 percent of his pass attempts, per PurdueSports.com.

In addition to Brees' significant on-field achievements, he also set his sights on excellence in the classroom. In his autobiography, he said that he had been getting good grades until the spring semester of his sophomore year. Unfortunately, he got a D in his Management 201 class. It was the first and only D he had ever received.

The D dropped his cumulative GPA to 3.2. However, Drew wanted to be an Academic All-American. To earn this distinction, the student-athlete must have a GPA of at least 3.25.

Proving that he was more than just a great athlete, Brees worked hard to earn that academic distinction by redeeming his grades. He worked hard on studying to make sure that he was going to make up for the first and only D he had ever received in his life as a student. Brees did so and kept making the Academic All-America Team throughout his entire stay in Purdue. Being an excellent student-athlete should be something every young boy should aspire to.

Entering Brees' junior season, experts already considered him to be a contender for the Heisman Trophy, the award given to the best player in college football. He told Reinmuth before the 1999 NCAA season that he did not try to think too much about it. If he did, it might have distracted him from performing well on the field. On the other hand, Purdue head football coach Joe Tiller told *The Chicago Tribune* that wins take precedence over Brees breaking every possible quarterback statistic in the college football ranks. Tiller even said he did not want Brees to throw 83 passes in a game ever again.

According to Reinmuth, Tiller had been looking at giving his running backs such as senior J. Crabtree and sophomore Dondre Johnson bigger roles in the offense. As a result, Brees' load would lighten.

His statistics reflected otherwise: he completed 337 of 554 pass attempts and threw for 3,909 yards and 25 touchdowns. The passing yardage was nearly identical to his production during his sophomore year. The more noticeable drop-off was in his touchdown passes, which decreased from 39 to 25. Nevertheless, he still led the Big Ten Conference with an average of 325.8 passing yards per game. He led the conference and placed third in the nation in average all-purpose yards per game with 340.5. He also added 177 rushing yards, which was good for third-best on the team. Brees scored four rushing touchdowns in 1999, per Purdue's official athletics website.

Brees started his junior year by throwing four touchdowns in the Boilermakers' season-opening 47-13 rout of the UCF Knights on September 4, 1999. He set Purdue's longest play from scrimmage when he threw a 99-yard touchdown pass to wide receiver Vinny Sutherland in a 31-23 win over the Northwestern

Wildcats on September 25th. It was the Boilermakers' fourth consecutive win. Brees completed 32 of 50 passes for 405 yards and three touchdowns. He earned Big Ten Player of the Week honors as a result.

Three weeks later, Brees went 40-of-57 passing for 509 yards and 5 touchdowns in a 52-28 win over the Michigan State Spartans at home. His passing yardage was good enough for third-best in school history for a single game. At that point in the season, the Boilermakers sported a 5-2 win-loss record.

Purdue would go on to lose three of their last five games to finish 7-5 in the 1999 NCAA season. It was good enough to earn a spot in the 1999 Outback Bowl against the Georgia Bulldogs on January 1, 2000. Organizers dubbed it the "First Sporting Event of the Millennium."

Brees started the game off hot. He threw two first-quarter touchdowns to wide receivers Chris Daniels and another one to Vinny Sutherland. Purdue led 19-0 after the first 15 minutes and would go on to post a 25-0 lead. However, Bulldogs quarterback Quincy Carter led a furious second-half comeback. Carter threw a touchdown pass to Randy McMichael in double coverage with 1:19 remaining to knot the count at 25 apiece.

The Bulldogs' offense clicked while the Boilermakers' offense sputtered.

The game eventually went to overtime for just the second overtime game in college bowl history, per OutbackBowl.com. The Boilermakers won the coin toss and managed to march the ball to the Bulldogs' 43-yard line. However, Purdue kicker Travis Dosch missed badly on his field-goal attempt. Had he won the game for the Boilermakers, they would have won their third consecutive bowl game. But it was not meant to be.

Carter led Georgia to Purdue's two-yard line, setting up a game-winning field goal attempt. Hap Hines' 19-yard attempt cleared the uprights. Final score: Georgia 28, Purdue 25.

Despite the heartbreaking loss, Brees earned the 1999 Outback Bowl MVP honors. He passed for 370 yards and 3 touchdowns, breaking or tying six Outback Bowl records in the process.[xv]

Brees also earned several more accolades after the 1999 NCAA season. The experts turned out to be right. Brees was a legitimate Heisman Trophy candidate and finished fourth in the voting. Wisconsin Badgers running back Ron Dayne eventually won the 1999 Heisman Trophy.

Brees won the 1999 Socrates Award–its first-ever recipient–for his performance in academics, athletics, and community service. He finished second in the voting for both the Davey O'Brien National Quarterback Award and Maxwell Award. Football News also named Brees to their 1999 Second Team All-American squad. The conference's coaches and media representatives selected Brees for the 1999 First Team All-Big Ten lineup. He was also Purdue's 1999 Male Athlete of the Year, according to the university's official athletics website.

Entering Brees' senior year in 2000, he had already converted 717 of 1,166 pass attempts and thrown for 8,124 yards and 64 touchdowns.[xvi] In two years as the Boilermakers' starting quarterback, he helped lead them to the 1998 Alamo Bowl. And he had already piled up a slew of accolades along the way.

Brees would further cement his legacy in the 2000 NCAA football season.

He led Purdue to two consecutive victories to start off the campaign. The Boilermakers shut out the Central Michigan Chippewas 48-0 on September 2, 2000. The week after, they routed the Kent State Golden Flashes, 48-10. In that game, Brees converted on 32 of 46 passes for 415 yards and 2 touchdowns. By doing so, he became the Boilermakers' all-time leader in career total offense and completions, per PurdueSports.com. Two weeks later, he went 33-of-49 passing for 409 yards and 2 touchdowns in a 38-24 win over the visiting Minnesota Golden Gophers. With those, Brees became Purdue's all-time leader in passing touchdowns and pass attempts. He also rushed for a career-best 88 yards in the game against Minnesota.

After the Penn State Nittany Lions had beaten the Purdue Boilermakers 22-20 on September 30th, the latter's record dropped to 3-2. Brees was far from satisfied. He felt that his team could have won against the Nittany Lions that week and the Notre Dame Fighting Irish two weeks earlier. He had reason to be upset—Purdue had lost those two games by a combined four points. And the schedule was not about to get any easier. The Boilermakers would face the sixth-ranked Michigan Wolverines, the 17th-ranked Northwestern Wildcats, and the 12th-ranked Ohio State Buckeyes over the next four weeks.

Brees and company squeaked by Michigan, 32-31, on a last-second field goal on October 7th. They beat Northwestern by 13 on the road the following week. Purdue ran their winning streak to three after they beat the Wisconsin Badgers, 30-24, on October 21st.

This set the stage for a matchup against the Buckeyes. It was the No. 12 Ohio State vs. No. 16 Purdue. The Boilermakers had not beaten the Buckeyes in seven previous matchups.[xvii] Brees wanted nothing more than to end that streak.

However, it was Ohio State that got off to a fast start on Purdue's home field. The Buckeyes led 20-10 entering the fourth quarter. At that point, Brees had not played well and had already thrown three interceptions. In Brees' autobiography, he blamed the deficit on Purdue's costly turnovers.

Nonetheless, the Boilermakers were still in it. They trimmed the deficit to three after Brees threw a touchdown pass to wide receiver John Standeford. After the Purdue defense stopped Ohio State, the former got the ball back. Brees threw a touchdown pass to Vinny Sutherland. Purdue not only overcame the 10-point deficit, but they also managed to grab a four-point lead to put the score at 24-20. There were six minutes left to play and the Purdue faithful were delirious with joy.

Brees and his teammates had one objective–to take care of the football at all costs. As Brees was about to pass, an Ohio State linebacker blitzed him up the middle. He wanted to throw the ball out of bounds to prevent the interception. Unfortunately, Brees slipped, which affected the trajectory of his pass. Instead of sailing out of bounds, the ball landed in the hands of Buckeyes safety Mike Doss. He was about to take it into the end zone for a pick-six when Brees knocked him out of bounds at Purdue's two-yard line. Ohio State eventually scored a touchdown several plays later to put them up by three, 27-24.

Brees felt the ghost of the 1998 Notre Dame game haunting him again. However, he had learned a valuable lesson in the Ohio State game two years later. He describes this in his autobiography:

"Instead of kicking myself or replaying the interception, I focused on the task at hand," he said. "One thing you learn quickly is that great quarterbacks must have short-term memories when it comes to things like this. Good or bad, you have to be able to finish a play, push it aside, and move on to the next one. You can never let a play from the past affect the present. Your job is to play in the moment."

Brees admitted that he felt the pressure in the ensuing Purdue possessions. It was a different kind of pressure–the kind which gives one an edge when it matters. Purdue offensive coordinator Jim Chaney called for a four-receiver set on second down. Brees emphasized that the quarterback goes to either of the first two receivers 90 percent of the time. The second option was the third receiver. The last option would be the outside receiver who runs a post route.

When Brees received the snap, he discovered that the Buckeyes had the first three receivers well covered. He then spotted his fourth option, wide receiver Seth Morales. No Ohio State defender was anywhere near him. Brees threw a perfect 64-yard pass that dropped right into the wide receiver's hands and Morales ran it in for the touchdown. Final score: Purdue 31, Ohio State 27. The Boilermakers had snapped the seven-game losing streak to their Big Ten Conference foes.

Brees knelt on the field and said a short prayer of thanks after the hard-earned victory. His linemen picked him up and congratulated him afterward.

One of those linemen was Matt Light, a future three-time Pro Bowl left tackle with the NFL's New England Patriots. "That is what makes you great! That is what makes you great!" he screamed in Brees' face.

Several months before Brees' autobiography came out, he recalled talking to former Ohio State head football coach Jim Tressel. In jest, the latter said he got the job because of Brees' performance in that game.

"I'll never forget what you did to Ohio State in that game in 2000," Tressel said. "In fact, I might not have this job if it weren't for that play."

"I guess everything happens for a reason, doesn't it, Coach?" Brees replied.

The year Perdue beat Ohio State, John Cooper was the Buckeyes' head football coach. They hired Tressel to replace him at the conclusion of the 2000 NCAA season.

After beating Ohio State, the Boilermakers extended their winning streak to four. They lost two of their last three games to finish the season with an 8-4 win-loss record.

Purdue made it to their fourth straight bowl appearance. The Boilermakers would next face the Washington Huskies in the Rose Bowl in Pasadena, California on January 2, 2001. The game would feature two of the nation's best quarterbacks, Drew Brees and Marques Tuiasosopo, who went on to play for the Raiders and the Jets and later became a coach for the UCLA Bruins.

The Boilermakers trailed 20-17 in the fourth quarter but their chances seemed to improve after Tuiasosopo left late in the third quarter due to an injured right shoulder. When he returned, however, he passed to wide receiver Todd Elstrom in the red zone. The latter enjoyed an eight-inch height advantage over Boilermakers cornerback Chris Clopton, who covered him. Elstrom literally leaped over Clopton for a touchdown and the Huskies lead widened to 27-17.

The Boilermakers tried to rally. However, Brees threw three straight incompletions once Purdue reached Washington's 24-yard line with 4:54 left in the game. To compound matters, kicker Travis Dorsch missed a 42-yard field goal which would have narrowed the gap to seven.

The two teams exchanged touchdowns in the waning moments, but it was not enough. The final score was Washington 34, Purdue 24.

Brees completed 23 of 39 passes for 275 yards and 2 touchdowns. Tuiasosopo complimented his counterpart after the game and said that the hard part of every game was that someone had to lose no matter how well-fought the matchup is and how good of a performance each competitor put on.[xviii]

Brees' accomplishments in 2000 backed up Tuiasosopo's statement. The former completed 309 of 512 passes (a 60.4 percent completion rate) in the 2000 NCAA season. He also passed for 3,668 yards, 26 touchdowns, and 12 interceptions.

Remarkably, Brees finished as the Boilermakers' second-leading rusher with 512 yards on 95 carries and 5 touchdowns. Only one Purdue quarterback had better stats on the ground. Bo Bobrowski rushed for 549 yards in 1973, per PurdueSports.com. Brees accounted for 4,189 yards of total offense in his senior year. He led the nation in average total offense (358.1 yards per game) in 2000.

At the end of Brees' collegiate career, he became Purdue and the Big Ten Conference's all-time leader in pass attempts (1,678), completions (1,026), passing yards (11,792), passing touchdowns (90), and total offense (12,292). He also became the all-time leader in career completion percentage (.611). Brees earned the distinction of being the only Big Ten Conference quarterback to record two games with at least 500 passing yards. He also had seven games with at least 400 passing yards, 16 games with at least 300, and 27 games with at least 250.

Brees proved once and for all that he was not just a typical quarterback gunslinger. He rushed for 14 touchdowns in his four-year stint with Purdue in West Lafayette, Indiana. By doing so, he tied the 14th all-time best record for any Purdue player regardless of position. Equally impressive were his 900 career rushing yards.

Finally, Brees won Big Ten Offensive Player of the Week eight times during his four-year collegiate career. It tied him with the Wisconsin Badgers' Ron Dayne–the 1999 Heisman Trophy Winner –for most ever in conference history.

It came as no surprise when the Purdue senior quarterback won the Maxwell Award. It gave him the distinction as the nation's top player. He also placed third in the Heisman Trophy voting behind the Florida State Seminoles' Chris Weinke and the Oklahoma Sooners' Josh Heupel.

Brees also continued to excel in the classroom. He finished his senior year with a 3.42 GPA and earned Academic All-American of the Year honors. He was the first Purdue player to get the nod in 11 years (offensive tackle Bruce Brineman won the award in 1989). The National Collegiate Scholar-Athlete and National Football Foundation also named him their National Collegiate Scholar-Athlete of the Year.

Brees' other accolades include Gannett News Service First Team All-American, Football News Third Team All-American, a finalist for Johnny Unitas Golden Arm Award, and a semifinalist for Davey O'Brien National Quarterback Award. He also received *The Chicago Tribune*'s Silver Football as Big Ten Most Valuable Player.

Drew Brees–the Austin, Texas native who once thought he could never excel in college football–earned countless awards and distinctions at the end of his stay at Purdue University. It was now time to take his game to the penultimate level–the National Football League.

# Chapter 4: Scouting Combine and 2001 NFL Draft

Just over a month after the loss to the Washington Huskies in the Rose Bowl, Drew Brees prepared himself for the biggest challenge of his life to date: entering the 2001 NFL Draft.

Before anything else, Brees needed bargaining power. For that, he had to decide who would represent him in negotiations.

According to *Sports Illustrated*'s Tim Layden, Brees was in Austin, Texas with his parents, Chip and Mina, in the first week of January 2001. Despite his parents' divorced status, they collaborated on one of their son's most important life decisions. Layden said that the Brees family had whittled their choices down to three agents before Drew's senior year at Purdue: IMG's Tom Condon, former Oakland Raiders safety Vann McElroy, and Leigh Steinberg.[xix]

Layden said that Brees met with Steinberg at a West Lafayette motel just before the Purdue Boilermakers' fall practice in August 2000. Steinberg unveiled an impressive portfolio of players he represented, including Drew Bledsoe, Jake Plummer, and Ryan Leaf. Brees liked what he saw. He also met with

McElroy and Steinberg at some point in the 2000 NCAA season.

Brees eventually decided to tap Condon because they struck a good connection, per *Sports Illustrated*. The Purdue standout also liked the fact that IMG had 35 offices nationwide. "Wherever I play, they'll be close," Brees said.

Brees also dismissed the notion that he chose Condon and IMG because the latter represented his friend, Indianapolis Colts quarterback Peyton Manning. Brees said that the two had not conversed in months. He also said he did not have Manning's new mobile number.

Layden said Brees prepared hard for the 2001 NFL Scouting Combine during his senior season at Purdue. He lifted weights four times a week. He did not want to put on mass, though; he wanted to increase his strength. Brees had trouble finding a teammate to spot for him because the other Boilermakers were equally busy lifting.

Brees also ran sprints five times a week. He incorporated other exercises to improve his running technique to boost his speed in the 40-yard dash, per Layden.

Brees participated in the NFL Scouting Combine at the Indianapolis Colts' RCA Dome in February 2001. General Managers, coaches, and scouts from all NFL teams were on hand for the annual event. They carefully evaluated the prospects' physical abilities, their overall state of health, and their ability fit into their team's system. For their part, the rookies go through all sorts of drills and check-ups.

Aside from Brees, the other notable collegiate prospects present were the Georgia Bulldogs' Quincy Carter, the TCU Horned Frogs' LaDainian Tomlinson, and the North Carolina Tar Heels' Alge Crumpler. Other collegiate stars on hand were the Arizona State Sun Devils' Todd Heap, the Oklahoma State Cowboys' Josh Heupel, and the Ole Miss Rebels' Deuce McAllister.

Brees had one of the best–if not the best–arms in all of college football during the previous NCAA season. Scouts and various personnel measured his arm strength with radar guns at the Scouting Combine. Brees revealed in his autobiography that he estimated his fastest throw at around 60 miles per hour. ESPN's Mel Kiper, Jr. wrote in his March 8, 2001, blog that Brees "may have lost some ground. While he was solid in the shorter areas, he struggled throwing the ball down the field."[xx]

The 6'0", 213-pound Brees' complete Scouting Combine results were as follows. He ran the 40-yard dash in 4.83 seconds, recorded a height of 32.0 inches in the vertical leap, a distance of 105 inches in the broad jump, ran 4.21 seconds in the shuttle drill, and 7.09 seconds in the three-cone drill. He did not participate in the 225-pound bench press.[xxi]

Aside from these exercises, the prospects also had to go through many interviews at the Scouting Combine. Brees remembered some of them that stood out. He had one with Kansas City Chiefs head coach Dick Vermeil. Brees confessed that he did not remember much because he had been gawking at Vermeil's Super Bowl ring. He wanted to earn one of his own.

Brees also spoke with San Diego Chargers offensive coordinator Norv Turner. "I could really feel his interest in me as a player and a person," Brees revealed in his book. "And that sense was confirmed when Norv, Chargers head coach Mike Riley, general manager John Butler, and a few other scouts came to Purdue a few weeks later to give me a personal workout."

Cincinnati Bengals president Mike Brown was also interested in Brees, per *Sports Illustrated*'s Tim Layden. This was despite the fact that the Bengals had drafted high-profile quarterback Akili

Smith third overall in 1999. Seattle Seahawks director of player personnel, John Schneider, was also interested in the Purdue standout.

Brees was not the least bit satisfied with his Scouting Combine performance. According to Layden, Brees drove his 1997 Chevy Tahoe–a gift from his father when he earned a Purdue scholarship–back to West Lafayette after the Scouting Combine. He spoke to his mom Mina as he drove.

"It wasn't great, Mom," Brees said. "It wasn't like I expected...I'm tired, really tired...I'm glad it's over."

Brees' Pro Day at Purdue University on March 21st was a chance for him to redeem himself.

He trained for the upcoming event with Larry Kennan, a former offensive coach in the NFL at the IMG Academies in Bradenton, Florida from March 11-18. Kennan served as the executive director of the NFL Coaches Association from 1998-2011. IMG tapped him to train Brees for his Pro Day, per Layden. Kennan had worked in that capacity for three years preparing NFL quarterback prospects before they strutted their wares for different pro teams.

Kennan also worked with Florida State Seminoles quarterback Chris Weinke (who later became the quarterbacks coach of the Los Angeles Rams) during his time with Brees. The two signal-callers each threw 100 times in a one-hour span daily on top of strength training and running.

The big day arrived. Drew Brees and his other Purdue Boilermakers teammates were ready for Pro Day on March 21st. Layden said representatives of seven NFL teams were on hand at Purdue University's Mollenkopf Center by 10:45 a.m. The Chargers' offensive coordinator, Norv Turner, was also there. He was the one Brees singled out in his autobiography as having a genuine interest in him during the 2001 NFL Scouting Combine. San Diego head coach Mike Riley accompanied Turner. The Chargers had the No. 1 pick in the 2001 NFL Draft. Could Drew Brees possibly go that high?

The team with the most representatives was the Kansas City Chiefs–they had president Carl Peterson, head coach Dick Vermeil, offensive coordinator Al Saunders, and quarterback coach Terry Shea. A few weeks before Brees' Pro Day workout, Kansas City lost starting quarterback Elvis Grbac to free agency. Layden theorized that the Chiefs wanted to leave no stone unturned in naming Grbac's successor. Brees–the 2000 Maxwell Award recipient–was one of the candidates.

The other teams which were present during Purdue's 2001 Pro Day were the Cincinnati Bengals, Buffalo Bills, Dallas Cowboys, Atlanta Falcons, and the Carolina Panthers, per *Sports Illustrated*.

According to Layden, Brees started his workout in an incredible fashion. He threw a total of 74 passes from different angles. His intended receivers dropped just two of them. Brees finished his exhibition just as he started it–in style. He threw two 70-yard passes which were right on target.

Five days later, Brees returned to Mollenkopf Center for the third day of his workout. This time, the Jacksonville Jaguars wanted to size him up. He exceeded their expectations.

On March 29th, the Chargers returned to the Purdue University campus to take another look at Brees. They also wanted to evaluate Virginia Tech Hokies star quarterback Michael Vick. Both did very well. At this point, no team had traded up to San Diego to get the No. 1 pick. Brees believed the Chargers would select Vick, per Layden.

Brees turned out to be incorrect in his assumption.

Purdue University sports information director Jim Vruggink informed Brees on April 20th–the day before the 2001 NFL

Draft–that the Chargers had traded their No. 1 pick to the Atlanta Falcons for the No. 5 pick, wide receiver and kickoff returner Tim Dwight, and several other draft choices. As expected, the Falcons made Vick the No. 1 overall draft pick that year.

Layden said the turn of events took Brees by surprise. He wanted San Diego to select him in the first round. In jest, Brees even said some other team should draft TCU Horned Frogs running back LaDainian Tomlinson before the Chargers got a chance to do so with the fifth overall pick.

"Three years ago, I had no idea who would pick me," Brees told *Sports Illustrated* in April 2001. "And I still don't. But I've got a funny feeling about San Diego."

Brees was so excited the day before the draft that he went to sleep at 2 a.m. and woke up just four hours later, per Layden. By 7:45 a.m. he would be playing golf at Purdue's Kampen Course to help him relax.

The 2001 NFL Draft took place at The Theater at MSG on April 21st. Brees would let the first hour of the draft pass by–he was on the sidelines watching the Purdue spring football game in West Lafayette, Indiana.

In Brees' autobiography, he said his girlfriend, Brittany Dudchenko (his college sweetheart whom he would marry two years later), flew his brother Reid in from Colorado so that they could watch the draft together. Drew Brees thought it was a pleasant surprise. As they were watching the draft, he fried some fish for them to eat.

Layden said Brees had gotten home just as San Diego nabbed Tomlinson with the fifth overall pick. Brees was stoic afterward. NFL officials had invited him to go to New York for the draft but he politely declined their offer because he did not want to be "the last guy in the green room."

When Brees was the New Orleans Saints' quarterback in 2014, he told *The Dan Patrick Show* (via ArrowheadPride.com) that he thought the Kansas City Chiefs would select him with the 12th overall pick.[xxii] As previously mentioned, the Chiefs were in dire need of a replacement for Elvis Grbac. However, Kansas City did not choose Brees. Instead, the Chiefs traded their first-round selection to their in-state rivals, the St. Louis Rams (now the Los Angeles Rams), for eight-year veteran quarterback Trent Green. After trading him, the Rams drafted Miami Hurricanes defensive tackle Damione Lewis with the 12th overall selection.

Dudchenko got more nervous as the picks went on. Just when the Miami Dolphins were about to make the 26th overall selection, Brees put the phone in front of the television.

Nearly half an hour later, Brees got his wish. The phone in front of his television rang. It was the Chargers. They were going to make Brees the 32nd overall pick.

San Diego was delighted to get Brees. Chargers head coach Mike Riley told *Sports Illustrated* that they wanted to trade up with the Dolphins for the 26th pick, but it did not materialize.

Brees said numerous sources–including his college coach Joe Tiller–told him Miami would draft him at No. 26. Tiller had a friend who worked for the Dolphins.

When the Dolphins passed up on Brees, he felt slighted. It was not so much that he did not become a first-round pick, it was because he felt that people had lied to him.

Now all the Chargers could do was hope Brees would still be available at number 32–the first pick of the second round.

Aside from getting the opportunity to work with Turner and company, Brees also cited several reasons why he was excited to play for the Chargers.

First, he would get to be on the same roster as San Diego quarterback Doug Flutie, someone whom he greatly admired. Brees felt he could learn so many things from the former Boston College Eagles legend who threw the famous Hail Mary pass in 1984 (Brees was just five years old that year) against the Miami Hurricanes.

Second, he would get to play with other big-name stars such as Tomlinson, linebacker Junior Seau, and safety Rodney Harrison.

Brees explained how he felt in the aftermath of the 2001 NFL Draft. "As I tried to wrap my brain around my new reality, I realized something," he said in his autobiography. "I could get stuck in disappointment because I hadn't gone in the first round like I'd envisioned, or I could be thankful I'd landed in the right place. Sometimes it's not how you get to your destination that's most important."

"The key is ending up in the right place–on the right team, in the right situation, with the right opportunity," he continued. "I felt that God had put me in San Diego for a reason. A new adventure was about to begin."

# Chapter 5: NFL Career with the San Diego Chargers

## 2001 NFL Season

Drew Christopher Brees had come full circle. He had dreams of becoming an MLB baseball player as a child, but instead, he ended up in Southern California to play quarterback for the NFL's San Diego Chargers.

Right from the start, Brees knew that he would serve as 39-year-old Doug Flutie's backup. He even had to compete with Dave Dickinson for the backup role.

Brees eventually won out. He played in his first-ever and only game in the 2001 NFL season on November 4th against the visiting Kansas City Chiefs. Entering the Week 8 showdown, the Chargers had won five of their first seven games. In sharp contrast, the Chiefs had lost six of their first seven.

Flutie had suffered a concussion in the second quarter after Chiefs defensive end Duane Clemons sacked him. Flutie finished with 61 passing yards and 1 interception. His time on the field was up.

Head coach Mike Riley tapped Brees to replace him. On this day, Brees' quarterback counterpart would be Trent Green. Almost seven months earlier, Brees thought the Chiefs would draft him 12th overall. Instead, Kansas City traded its pick to acquire Green from the St. Louis Rams. It was clear the Chiefs believed they had a better chance of succeeding with Green as their quarterback. For Brees, his first NFL game was payback time.

He was unfazed the moment he took the field. He led San Diego to four consecutive scoring drives in the second half. Kansas City dictated the game's tempo from the very beginning. Brees changed that when he threw a touchdown pass to wide receiver Freddie Jones with 6:10 left in the match. Brees threw the defense off with a timely pump fake. After Jones hauled the ball into the end zone, Brees pumped his fist and celebrated his first-ever NFL touchdown pass with his teammates. At that point, the Chargers were ahead 20-19–their first lead of the contest.

Green and running back Priest Holmes countered with a 71-yard drive in the waning moments. It culminated in Chiefs fullback Tony Richardson's one-yard touchdown with 1:26 remaining.

Brees had a chance to win the game for San Diego. His team spotted the ball on Kansas City's 32-yard line with no timeouts left. The officials whistled the Chiefs for a personal foul. It resulted in the Chargers moving the ball to midfield. However, Brees made an illegal forward pass on third down with 13 seconds on the game clock and his team ended up losing the game. Brees said later on that those were plays that work in college but not in the professional level. xxiii

Brees filled in admirably for the injured Flutie. The latter converted on 15 of 27 pass attempts for 221 yards and 1 touchdown.

Flutie told ESPN that he blacked out when he hit his head on the field after Clemons sacked him. He regained consciousness at halftime and described Brees' first game with a few choice words, saying that the young man seemingly knew what he was doing out there.

Brees considered Flutie to be his mentor. The young quarterback looked up to the veteran because of how intensely he played. The latter knew it was this passion which carried Flutie through more than 20 grueling seasons as a professional quarterback. Brees lauded Flutie for his tough-as-nails attitude. No matter how hard the defense tried to knock him down, he would always be one step ahead. Brees recalled an incident during the Chargers' training camp in 2002 when a teammate on the defense ran into Flutie on the sideline. He separated his shoulder as a result. Nonetheless, he stood back up as if it were nothing. He did not let anyone know about it until two weeks later.

Flutie gave his young protégé sound advice early during the 2002 NFL season. "I've learned to never take myself out of a game and to never let someone else take you out of a game," he said in Brees' autobiography. "Do whatever you can to prevent injury, but if you do get hurt, fight through whatever you can. Never give your backup the opportunity to see the field because you might not get back out there again."

Despite Brees being Flutie's backup, he took the advice to heart. He knew the old warrior cared for him deeply. He never saw Brees as a threat. Because of the mutual respect they had for one another, they forged a bond that lasts to this very day.

Brees' performance in Week 8 was one of the few bright spots in what turned out to be a dismal season for the Chargers. The loss to the Chiefs started a nine-game slide which dropped them to 5-11. During that tailspin, the Chargers lost by an average of just six points (only three of those nine straight losses were by double digits). San Diego finished dead last in the AFC West.

The Chargers fired Mike Riley after the season and hired Marty Schottenheimer as their new head coach.

## 2002 NFL Season

Brees and his fiancée Brittany Dudchenko returned from their European vacation during the 2002 offseason. When the San Diego Chargers introduced Marty Schottenheimer as their new head coach, Brees liked the hire from the beginning. Schottenheimer also brought in Cam Cameron, his son Brian, and Pete Carmichael as his assistants.

Brees respected his new coach's approach. Schottenheimer repeatedly discussed how great quarterbacks of the past such as Bernie Kosar, Joe Montana, and Rich Gannon played. Brees gave him credit for toughening him up mentally and emotionally. He also remembered how emotional Schottenheimer got during the Chargers' team meetings. More often than not, he would cry because of his passion for the game of football.

Brees also recalled several instances when Schottenheimer unintentionally spat in his face when he sat in the front row during team meetings. That was how passionate the veteran coach was.

"I'd still run through a wall for him," Brees wrote in his autobiography eight years after he first met Schottenheimer.

The new man in charge declared the starting quarterback job a tossup between Brees and Doug Flutie. Whoever worked harder would earn it.

Brees eventually won out. He honestly thought the competition was dead even. However, he felt the age difference (Brees was just 23 years old while Flutie was already 40) was the telling factor. Schottenheimer decided to pass the baton to the younger quarterback with a tremendous upside. Brees wound up starting every game for San Diego in the 2002 NFL season.

Brees played in his first NFL start on September 8, 2002, in a road game against the Cincinnati Bengals. He converted on 15 of 19 pass attempts for 160 yards, 2 touchdowns, and no interceptions in the 34-6 blowout victory.[xxiv] Fellow second-year player LaDainian Tomlinson added 114 yards on 21 carries. Brees told the Associated Press (via ESPN) that he did not feel nervous at all. He was simply relaxed the entire game instead of feeling the jitters and nerves that other players might have felt when in the same position as he was.[xxv]

Brees orchestrated a 15-play, 95-yard touchdown drive in the second quarter. San Diego led 20-0 at the half and never looked back. Their defense also held, limiting the Bengals' possession to just 7:53 in the first half. Chargers linebacker Junior Seau also held star Cincinnati running back Corey Dillon to just 10 rushing yards. At the end of the game, Seau praised Brees for his poise.

With the win, Marty Schottenheimer was off to a good start in his coaching career with the Chargers.

San Diego also won their next three games. Brees threw for an average of almost 150 yards per game during that streak.

After the Chargers had lost to the Denver Broncos 26-9 in Week 5, they beat the Kansas City Chiefs and Oakland Raiders to run their record up to 6-1. Brees threw for 319 yards and 2 touchdowns in the 35-34 win over Kansas City. Despite the fact that he threw two interceptions, it was arguably his best game of the season's first half. Things were looking good in San Diego.

And then, just like the year before, the bottom fell out. The Chargers went 2-7 in their last nine games to finish the season at 8-8. They missed the postseason for the seventh consecutive year.

Brees had a brief run-in with Schottenheimer in the Week 15 game against the Buffalo Bills.

Brees knew about Flutie's history with the Bills; they were the latter's former team. During Flutie's time in Western New York from 1998-2000, Buffalo had a quarterback controversy. Half of the team wanted him while the other half wanted Rob Johnson. When the Chargers signed Flutie in 2001, he wanted no part of that anymore.

San Diego took on Buffalo on December 15, 2002. According to Brees' autobiography, Schottenheimer told him he was going to pull him out in the fourth quarter for Flutie. The Chargers were losing at that point. Nobody on the team had played well, including Brees. Schottenheimer believed Flutie could spark the team, at least for this game.

Brees remembered Flutie's advice about not letting your backup see the field. The former refused to come out. In the end, the head coach had his way. Brees accepted Schottenheimer's decision and the Chargers lost, 20-13.

At season's end, Brees had thrown for 3,284 yards, 17 touchdowns, and 16 interceptions for a passer rating of 76.9.

Brees' 2002 season had its share of ups and downs. Despite missing the playoffs, the Chargers added three more wins to the win column. Brees saw that as progress. He believed this would continue in 2003.

## 2003 NFL Season

Brees hoped the Chargers' trend of starting strong and finishing weak over the past two seasons would finally come to an end in 2003. But unfortunately, it did not. The 2003 San Diego Chargers were a bad team from start to finish.

They got off to a woeful 0-5 start and lost by an average of 12 points during that slide. Brees put up average numbers, throwing for seven touchdowns and seven interceptions.

He said in his book that the lowest point of the 2003 season–and his NFL career up to that point–was the Week 9 road game against the Chicago Bears. Entering the contest, San Diego was a dismal 1-6.

In sharp contrast to Brees' first game as an NFL starting quarterback against the Cincinnati Bengals the year before, he was very tight in the match against Chicago. He forced the issue on just about every possession and threw several incompletions to wide receiver Tim Dwight. In the Chargers' 20-7 loss, Brees completed 7 of 15 passes for just 49 yards and 1 interception. He was a complete non-factor.

Marty Schottenheimer stated the obvious when he benched Brees for 41-year-old Doug Flutie.

Greg Olson was Brees' quarterback coach with the Purdue Boilermakers. When the Chargers faced the Bears, Olson served as Chicago's quarterback coach. He felt sorry for Brees after the game. He consoled his former protégé, hoping to lift his spirits after a disheartening performance during a very dismal season. Brees fought back the tears. Despite the setback, he told Olson, "I'm going to be a great player in this league someday."

Olson wholeheartedly agreed.

Brees had to wait before his prediction came true–Schottenheimer benched him for the next five games.

Brees saw this as a positive. It was an opportunity for him to re-evaluate his perspective and attitude toward his coaches and teammates. He became an impromptu coach and motivator on the sideline. Brees sized up the defense and gave Flutie advice on what the offense's best options were. Brees' passion for the game returned with a vengeance.

Schottenheimer started Brees again in the Week 15 game against the Green Bay Packers. Brees responded by throwing a season-high 363 yards to go along with 2 touchdowns in the 38-21 loss.

Brees engineered a short-lived comeback against the Pittsburgh Steelers in Week 16. The Chargers were down 21-0. They responded by scoring the next 17 points to narrow the gap to 4. But San Diego could not gain any further momentum when Brees fumbled in the third quarter. He then threw an interception on the Chargers' next possession and Schottenheimer benched him again. San Diego lost 40-24.

Schottenheimer and Brees engaged in a heated shouting match in the hallway after the game. Brees said they did not call each other names—it was just two passionate football people going at it.

Schottenheimer put Brees at ease when he told him he would still be the starter. When Brees turned the ball over three times against Pittsburgh, Schottenheimer yanked him out. The Chargers head coach did what he had to do. The Chargers won their final game of the 2003 NFL season against the Oakland Raiders, 21-14.

San Diego finished with a lowly 4-12 win-loss record. The team missed the postseason for the eighth consecutive year. Brees threw for 2,108 yards, 11 touchdowns, and 15 interceptions for a 67.5 passer rating in 11 games.[xxvi]

He felt the season was not a total disappointment, per his autobiography. He learned a lot from his disappointments and also strengthened his faith and relationship with Chargers' team chaplain, Shawn Mitchell.

However, Brees started to have doubts about his future in San Diego. Former Chargers general manager John Butler tragically succumbed to lymphoma–a cancer of the immune system–in April 2003. He was the executive that had drafted Brees two years ago. San Diego had a new general manager–A.J. Smith.

Brees knew that Smith had doubts about the Chargers' chances with him as the quarterback.

San Diego offensive coordinator Cam Cameron spoke with Brees after the 2003 season. He confided in Brees: The Chargers' brass was going to bring in a new quarterback. Cameron wanted to be blunt with him–upper management did not trust Brees as the team's quarterback. Cameron, Schottenheimer, and the rest of the coaching staff felt otherwise. He also added that Brees should be prepared to compete hard for his starting role.

Brees thanked Cameron for telling him. The latter knew he had to work harder than ever to get his job back.

## 2004 NFL Season

The San Diego Chargers were thinking about changing their quarterback situation in the 2004 NFL season. However, Cam Cameron was on Drew Brees' side. He believed the fourth-year man could improve despite his mediocre showing in 2003. Cameron also wanted to help Brees in any way he could.

Enter Tom House.

Cameron introduced House to Brees in the offseason. House was a famous MLB pitching coach with an extensive resume. He worked with the Houston Astros and the San Diego Padres as well as the Nippon Professional Baseball's Chunichi Dragons and Chiba Lotte Marines in Japan. When he met Brees, he was a member of the USC Trojans' baseball staff.

According to Brees' book, House did not just specialize in the physical development of an athlete. He also worked on the emotional and mental aspects of participating in professional athletics and dealt with the athlete's nutrition, sleeping habits, and attitude.

House introduced Brees to several joint integrity exercises to strengthen his back-side shoulder and core muscles. The two would train regularly at 5 a.m. for four months.

House also suggested Brees take a food allergy test to shore up his nutrition. It turned out Brees was allergic to nuts, dairy, wheat, gluten, and eggs. To his astonishment, he felt stronger and slept better when he made adjustments to his diet. House then introduced Brees to a visualization technique specialist to improve the mental aspect of his game. The latter felt that the sessions boosted his confidence and, as a result, he expected to know how a play will develop during games once the season started.

House also suggested Brees take a "star profile," a personality test for athletes. The results revealed he could be outgoing or reserved depending on the situation. That told Brees he needed to know when to be more assertive as a leader in game situations.

He was now ready to fight for his position as the San Diego Chargers' starting quarterback.

San Diego, after finishing 4-12 in 2003, had the No. 1 overall pick in the 2004 NFL Draft. Many expected the Chargers to select Ole Miss Runnin' Rebels quarterback Eli Manning, the son of former New Orleans Saints quarterback Archie and younger brother of Indianapolis Colts quarterback Peyton Manning.

Eli Manning stirred controversy before the draft when he said he did not want to go to San Diego. Many experts believed it was because of the Chargers' incompetence or the way he fit with the New York Giants, who had the fourth overall pick. It did not matter in the end, and the Chargers still made Manning the first overall pick in 2004.

An hour later, San Diego traded Manning to the Giants for North Carolina State Wolfpack quarterback Philip Rivers and three draft picks. Brees remembered hopping on his treadmill right after the trade. He knew he had his work cut out for him, per his autobiography.

Brees made it clear that he and Rivers were friends from the get-go. They had a mutual respect. However, Brees was not about to let Rivers take his job away from him. Doug Flutie's advice in 2001 resonated yet again.

Brees requested a players-only meeting after the first training camp session in 2004. He talked to his teammates about their goals, leadership, commitment, and adversity. He even shared some motivational quotes he had collected. At that precise moment, Drew Brees made it clear to his teammates that he was their leader on the field.

It came as no surprise when Chargers head coach Marty Schottenheimer named him as the starter. Flutie served as the main backup while Rivers was the third-string quarterback.

Brees' 2004 season got off to a superb start–he went 17-of-24 passing for 209 yards and no interceptions in a 27-20 road win over the Houston Texans in Week 1.[xxvii]

In the Chargers' next game against the New York Jets, Brees ran into a roadblock.

Jets safety Jon McGraw and linebacker Jonathan Vilma blitzed Brees in the third quarter. Brees remembered hitting his head on the Qualcomm Stadium field. The tenacious blow chipped three of his teeth and he also suffered a concussion.

San Diego's coaching staff sat him out for the rest of the game, and Flutie came in for him. Brees heard afterward that Chargers general manager A.J. Smith and his crew were upset because they wanted Rivers–the rookie they had traded for–to see some action. The Jets won 34-28. Brees finished with 146 passing yards, 1 touchdown, and 2 interceptions.

After the Week 3 loss to the Denver Broncos, Schottenheimer told Brees he had upgraded Rivers to the primary backup spot.

"I heard the underlying message–I was on a short leash," Brees said in his autobiography. "If I didn't play well, I would be pulled. Philip would be going in. I gave Marty a look that said, 'I don't care who the backup quarterback is because he's never going to see the field.'"

Brees said he had a heart-to-heart talk with Chargers fullback Lorenzo Neal during this trying time and Neal challenged him. He thought Brees had what it took to be a Pro Bowl quarterback. Now he had to prove it once and for all.

Brees would suffer another setback in the Week 4 game against the Tennessee Titans on October 3rd. Titans defensive tackle Rien Long sacked Brees in the second quarter. Chargers' physicians informed Brees that he had separated the AC joint in his shoulder.

Neal encouraged Brees to tough out the injury. He did, and led San Diego to several touchdown drives to secure the 38-17 win at home. The victory upped the Chargers' record to 2-2 on the season. Brees completed 16 of his 20 passes for 206 yards, 3 touchdowns, and no interceptions.

A renewed Brees resulted in a rejuvenated Chargers group–San Diego won 10 of their next 12 games. The Chargers beat the opposition by an average of 12.5 points during that tear. They were a far cry from the San Diego teams of old, and it was all thanks to Drew Brees.

Brees finished the 2004 NFL season with 3,159 passing yards, but more importantly, he significantly improved his touchdown-to-interception ratio. He threw for 27 touchdowns with 7 interceptions in 2004. The year before, he had 11 touchdowns and 15 interceptions. It was a remarkable turnaround.

Even before the season began, Neal called Brees "PB," which stood for "Pro Bowl." Neal turned out to be right–Brees made it to his first-ever Pro Bowl. He also won 2004 NFL Comeback Player of the Year honors. It was a season to remember for Drew Brees.

He also made it to his first NFL postseason appearance. With a 12-4 regular-season record, the Chargers drew a bye in the Wild Card round. They faced the New York Jets in the divisional round at San Diego's Qualcomm Stadium on January 8, 2005.

The Chargers struck first when Brees threw a terrific 26-yard touchdown pass to wide receiver Keenan McCardell in the second quarter. McCardell's over-the-shoulder catch was just as spectacular–he managed to haul the ball into the end zone just before he fell out of bounds. The officials initially ruled it incomplete, but Schottenheimer's challenge overturned it. San Diego 7, NY Jets 0.[xxviii]

Moments later, the Chargers' head coach got an unsportsmanlike conduct penalty after he protested a missed call against San Diego punter Mike Scifres. The Jets then spotted the ball on the Chargers' 37-yard line. Five plays later, New York quarterback Chad Pennington threw a 13-yard touchdown pass to tight end Anthony Becht to tie things up at 7.

Pennington then gave the Jets their first lead of the game when he connected with wide receiver Santana Moss in the third quarter for a 14-7 lead. They soon added a field goal to increase the score by 10 points.

The Chargers then scored on a field goal in the fourth quarter. Brees threw a one-yard touchdown pass to tight end Antonio Gates to tie the score with 11 seconds left in the ballgame and send the game into overtime.

San Diego had a chance to win it with 4:19 left in overtime. However, kicker Nate Kaeding missed a 40-yard field goal attempt. The Jets capitalized on the missed opportunity. Their kicker, Doug Brien, made a 28-yard field goal with just five seconds remaining in the extra session. Final score: NY Jets 20,

San Diego Chargers 17. The latter's postseason had ended on a sad note.

Brees completed 31 of his 42 pass attempts for 319 yards, 2 touchdowns, and 1 interception. Despite the loss to the Jets, the Chargers had made great strides. They won their division and made their first postseason appearance in nine years. San Diego expected bigger things in 2005.

## 2005 NFL Season

The San Diego Chargers made huge strides in the 2004 NFL season. Their starting quarterback and leader, Drew Brees, became a certified Pro Bowler. They were looking forward to another successful campaign in 2005.

The Chargers put the franchise player tag on Brees in 2005. This meant that he was on a one-year deal with his salary based on the earnings of the league's top five quarterbacks. San Diego had the option of releasing him, putting the franchise tag on him again or giving him a long-term contract after the season.

With second-year quarterback Philip Rivers playing behind him, would this be his last year in San Diego? The stakes were very high. Brees had to be at the top of his game and lead the Chargers deep into the postseason.

Unfortunately, San Diego did not get off to a good start. The Chargers lost their first two games of the 2005 NFL season. They went on to post a 5-4 win-loss record before their bye week. Brees put up some decent numbers during that stretch with 14 touchdowns and 8 interceptions. His best game before the bye week was a 28-20 win against the Kansas City Chiefs on October 30, 2005. Brees went 25-of-43 passing for 324 yards, 3 touchdowns, and 1 interception.[xxix]

Tight end Antonio Gates caught all three of Brees' touchdown passes. He finished with 145 receiving yards on 10 receptions. Brees praised Gates, who also happened to be a former college basketball player, after the game. He told the Associated Press that he thought Gates was someone who you really could not tackle due to his power. On top of that, he also had a unique ability to catch the ball really well and was a gifted player at his position due to his combination of skill and physical capabilities.[xxx]

Brees picked up where he left off in the Week 11 game against the Buffalo Bills. He connected on 28 of his 33 passes for a spectacular 84.8 percent accuracy. Brees threw touchdown passes to four different receivers–Antonio Gates, Keenan McCardell, Eric Parker, and Lorenzo Neal. He finished with 339 yards and no interceptions in the 48-10 rout over Buffalo.

The crucial win propelled San Diego's win-loss record to 6-4. The Chargers would continue to gain momentum as the season wore on. They won four of their next six games to improve to 9-6 on the season.

It set the stage for the Week 17 game against the Denver Broncos, a game that became the turning point in Drew Brees' career with the San Diego Chargers.

At this point in the season, the Chargers were a longshot to make the playoffs. The Broncos led the AFC West with a 12-3 record heading into the game against San Diego. The Chiefs–another AFC West foe–had the same record as the Chargers (9-6) heading into Week 17.

Brees recalled that many experts and Chargers fans had different opinions on the starting quarterback position. Some wanted him to stay, and others wanted to go in a different direction with Rivers. The game against the Chargers would weigh heavily on this hot-button topic.

The Broncos stifled the Chargers' offense well into the second quarter and were up 14-0. At that point, Brees dropped back to pass deep in his end zone. Broncos free safety John Lynch sacked Brees, knocking the ball loose in the process. As Brees dived to recover the ball (an act he labeled a "cardinal sin" in his autobiography), he dislocated his right shoulder.

"Unfortunately, I didn't get the ball," he said in his book. "And even worse, after the dust had settled, my right shoulder was out of its socket. My arm stuck out to the side as if I were resting it on a fence post."

Brees did not feel anything in his right arm as he walked to the sideline. Different thoughts crept into his mind: Was this his last season with the Chargers? Would he play the next season? Would he play football again?

Brees knew it was another test of faith. He tried to be optimistic but was realistic at the same time. San Diego went on to lose to Denver, 23-7. The Chargers finished with a 9-7 record but missed out on the postseason.

Chargers general manager A.J. Smith–who never really praised Brees' games–reached out to his quarterback before the latter visited orthopedic surgeon Dr. James Andrews in Alabama. He told Brees that he should not worry about his contract because they were already guaranteeing him a long-term deal. Instead of focusing on his future with the team, the GM told the quarterback that he should be focusing on taking care of his arm so that he could return healthy. That was the assurance that Drew Brees needed.

Brees went to see Dr. Andrews in Alabama. After several tests, Dr. Andrews' prognosis on Brees' dislocated shoulder was grim. He revealed that Brees had torn his labrum and damaged his rotator cuff as well. If Brees underwent arthroscopic surgery, his projected recovery period was eight months. If he opted to have a traditional shoulder surgery, the recovery time would be around ten months. Dr. Andrews went for the first option. He said Brees' rehabilitation was the key to how fast he would be able to return to the field.

Brees and Dudchenko stayed with the latter's parents in Alabama while he was recovering from off-season shoulder surgery. His father-in-law drove him to rehab with Kevin Wilk, one of the nation's best physical therapists, every morning at 7:30. It was a tough time for Brees. He needed help to execute menial tasks such as brushing his teeth and getting dressed and also had trouble sleeping due to the excruciating pain. Nonetheless, he pored over Biblical scripture to deepen his faith, per his autobiography.

A month after Brees underwent surgery, Smith lived up to his promise. He gave Brees a long-term deal, but Brees was far from satisfied. Even though the Chargers had guaranteed that they were going to give their quarterback a long-term deal, it was a disappointing one. Drew Brees described it as a deal for a backup instead of a contract for a Pro Bowl quarterback.

But it really was never about the money for Drew Brees. For him, he felt disrespected by the notion that he was only worth as much as a backup. The disrespect he felt was what ultimately made him realize that he was not as valued by the team as he originally thought he was.

Brees read between the lines. He knew he was not the Chargers' answer at quarterback. As a professional football player, he said he needed the organization's support at that very moment. He felt that he did not get it, and that hurt him a great deal.

Brees also felt that he had not yet reached his peak. He could still prove he was a Pro Bowler and the man who would lead the Chargers to a Super Bowl title. However, his shoulder injury showed otherwise.

His agent, IMG's Tom Condon, negotiated with Smith and the Chargers for several weeks. Brees thought it was a futile effort— he knew his time in San Diego had ended. He expected to be a free agent.

He remembered as many as eight other teams showed interest. Their offers–which were primarily for backup quarterbacks–did not satisfy him. In the end, he whittled his options down to two teams: the Miami Dolphins and New Orleans Saints.

Brees' line of reasoning was simple. Miami and New Orleans were the only two squads that felt he was a starting quarterback in the NFL. Condon helped his client weigh the pros and cons of each option when the league's free-agency period began in March 2006.

Condon said Brees had to consider that New Orleans had just experienced Hurricane Katrina, the most devastating natural disaster in United States history. Seven months after the hurricane ravaged the Big Easy in August 2005, roughly 80 percent of the city was still underwater. That forced the Saints to relocate to San Antonio, Texas. There were even rumors that they would move to a different city permanently. The Saints also had a new coaching staff. Head coach Sean Payton had an unproven track record, and what was more was that Condon predicted team president and general manager Mickey Loomis would have a hard time luring big-name players to New Orleans. In his autobiography, even Brees thought the Saints were a "dead-end organization."

As for Miami, Condon told Brees it was a great city to play in. It had a great atmosphere and climate. He also pointed out the Dolphins were known for their winning tradition. In contrast to Peyton in New Orleans, Miami head coach Nick Saban was known to be a winner. Condon also held the other Dolphins coaches such as offensive coordinator Mike Mularkey and quarterback coach Jason Garrett in high regard. To top it all off, Miami offensive line coach Hudson Houck had worked with Brees in San Diego.

Brees and Condon agreed they would visit both cities. They met first with Dolphins general manager Randy Mueller and head coach Nick Saban for breakfast in Birmingham, Alabama. Brees recalled that it was uneventful. Saban told Brees and his wife about the organization's reputation and how great the city of Miami is for raising a family.

After the breakfast meeting with Saban and Mueller, Brees and his wife flew to New Orleans. Brees met Saints head coach Sean Payton at an Arby's drive-through in Birmingham several weeks earlier. The former said he felt the New Orleans organization had a genuine interest in him, per his autobiography.

Loomis, his wife Melanie, Payton and his wife Beth, quarterbacks coach Pete Carmichael, and other members of Payton's staff joined the Brees couple for dinner in New Orleans.

The following day, Payton and staff showed Brees his highlight reel with the Chargers. They discussed how he fit into their offensive scheme and how much input he would be able to give. Brees felt the Saints believed in and wanted him at that very moment. Payton valuing his input made all the difference. He then took the Brees couple on a tour of New Orleans–or what was left of it–in the aftermath of Hurricane Katrina.

A few days later, Brees and his wife met with the Dolphins' brass for dinner in Miami–owner Wayne Huizenga, head coach Nick Saban, the other coaches, and their wives were all present. Brees felt it was similar to the treatment they received in New Orleans–until the Dolphins asked him to undergo physicals on his shoulder with their team doctor the following day. He spent six hours with the Miami physicians. Deep inside, he felt like he was at the 2001 NFL Scouting Combine all over again. Worse, he felt the Dolphins had doubts about his abilities after the shoulder injury. Brees thought it was the same way the Chargers felt about him after they tendered their so-called long-term deal.

When Brees returned to Birmingham, Condon anticipated the Dolphins would call the following morning and inform them that there were problems with Brees' physicals. As expected, the Dolphins called. Condon was right all along.

Later on, Brees called Dolphins head coach Nick Saban. Saban told him that Miami would find itself in a tight financial position if the team tendered Brees a starting quarterback's salary, and it turned out he would not get to play much because of his ailing shoulder. Brees then asked Saban if he believed he could come back and lead the Dolphins to a Super Bowl title.

Saban paused.

"That was really all I needed to hear," Brees said in his book. "His pause told me everything."

Brees then thanked Saban for the opportunity. He told him he would be playing for the New Orleans Saints and hung up.

# Chapter 6: NFL Career with New Orleans Saints

## 2006 NFL Season

Brees felt confident that he had made the right choice when he committed to the New Orleans Saints in 2006. He also had his share of fears and doubts about his shoulder injury and the fact that his new team and the city of New Orleans had to start from scratch.

He received some good news from his orthopedic surgeon, Dr. James Andrews, almost four months after he injured his shoulder. He had cleared Brees to start throwing again. His first throw involved more of a pushing motion than a throwing one and was a far cry from the usual bombs he threw inside the pocket. Brees and his physical therapist Kevin Wilk worked eight to nine hours a day on different strengthening exercises to boost the recovery process. Their resilience would pay off as Brees slowly started to regain the strength he had lost. He even used the visualization techniques he learned early in his career with the San Diego Chargers to improve his throwing technique and accuracy.

Brees reported for Saints training camp in Jackson, Mississippi in July 2006. He pegged his recovery at 70 percent, per his autobiography. He eventually started throwing 120 balls on the fifth day of camp. Brees joined the likes of nose guard Hollis Thomas as well as linebackers Scott Fujita, Mark Simoneau, and Scott Shanle as new members of the Saints. There were a lot of new faces on the roster. New Orleans hoped they would help improve the team's abysmal 3-13 showing in the 2005 NFL season.

Brees' first game in a Saints uniform was on September 10, 2006, against the Cleveland Browns. A few minutes before kickoff, he initiated a players-only meeting in the locker room. He distributed sheets with the word "FAITH" (an acronym which stood for "Fortitude, Attitude, Integrity, Trust, and Humility") written on them. As the leader of the Saints, Brees wanted to set the tone for the rest of the season. It was a new beginning for New Orleans a little over a year after Hurricane Katrina nearly wiped out the city.

Brees completed 16 of 30 passes for 176 yards and 1 touchdown in the 19-14 season-opening road victory over Cleveland.[xxxi] Saints rookie running back Reggie Bush added 141 all-purpose yards. Head coach Sean Payton had clinched his first victory as an NFL head coach. For his part, Brees had won for the first time as a New Orleans Saint. He hoped that this would be the start of something bigger.

The Saints traveled north to face Brett Favre and the Green Bay Packers in Week 2. The rejuvenated Brees threw for 353 yards, 2 touchdowns, and 1 interception in the 34-27 win. Green Bay got off to a 13-0 lead in the first half. However, New Orleans fought back with two touchdowns—one by running back Deuce McAllister and another one by wide receiver Devery Henderson—in the second quarter. The Saints led 14-13 at the half. They then added two more touchdowns in the fourth quarter to secure the improbable victory.

The following week, the Saints were going to play a regular-season game in New Orleans in front of their loyal fans for the first time since December 26, 2004, after they had temporarily relocated to San Antonio, Texas in the 2005 NFL season because of Hurricane Katrina.

In his autobiography, Brees revealed that the Saints sold just 32,000 of the 70,000 season tickets in the Louisiana Superdome, their home stadium. To his astonishment, they sold out the Week 3 ESPN Monday Night Football game against their NFC South nemesis, the Atlanta Falcons, months in advance.

Brees explained in his book what that game against the Falcons meant to the city of New Orleans. "What made the night so memorable, though, was not the rivalry," he said. "It was what the game symbolized. Over the past year, the city had put up with rumors, snide remarks, put-downs, and conjecture that New Orleans was dead. With a city that is below sea level and a levee system in need of being completely revamped, there was the very real threat of hurricanes coming through the Gulf (of Mexico) each year and wreaking damage. Some said, 'Just let it go. There are too many bad memories. The cause is hopeless.' The people of New Orleans didn't buy that, and neither did the team. This was our home. With this game, we were going to show everyone the passion and emotion that New Orleans possessed. The team was rising, the people were rising, and the city was rising. On Monday night, we would show the world that New Orleans was not only coming back, we were coming back stronger."

The game had so much hype around it. Famous recording artists the Goo Goo Dolls, U2, and Green Day performed their rendition of "The Saints Are Coming" before kickoff. It also marked Drew Brees' first time playing in New Orleans as a member of the Saints.

It was all New Orleans from the opening kickoff. The offense could do no wrong and the defense held strong from the get-go as well. Saints special teamer Steve Gleason blocked the punt of the Falcons' Michael Koenen in the first quarter. Another member of New Orleans' special teams, Curtis Deloatch, recovered the ball in the end zone for a touchdown. In his autobiography, Brees described the home crowd's reaction as "the loudest one-time roar I have ever heard in a stadium."

The Saints went on to win 23-3. Drew Brees connected on 20 of 28 passes with 191 passing yards. At 3-0, New Orleans had already tied its win total in 2005. Better yet, it was just Week 3 of the regular season. It was a different New Orleans Saints team; there was no doubt about it.

The Saints went 7-6 the rest of the way to finish with a 10-6 record for the 2006 NFL season—a seven-game turnaround from the season before. It was also enough for New Orleans to earn the No. 2 seed in the NFC and a first-round bye. Brees finished with 4,418 passing yards, 26 touchdowns, and 11 interceptions in 2006. He also earned his second Pro Bowl selection in his first year with the New Orleans Saints. The painful memories of the season-ending shoulder injury with the San Diego Chargers the year before were now a thing of the past. Brees hoped that he would continue to overachieve in the postseason.

First up for the Saints were the Philadelphia Eagles in the divisional round. According to Brees' book, it was just the second time the Saints had made it to the divisional round. It was also their first time to host a divisional-round game. Despite missing the services of starting quarterback Donovan McNabb due to an injury, the Eagles were playing well with Jeff Garcia leading the way.

It was a tight game from the beginning. Philadelphia led 14-13 at the half. The Eagles threatened to break the game wide open when running back Brian Westbrook ran for a 62-yard touchdown in the third quarter to make it 21-13 in their favor. But Saints running back Deuce McAllister countered with a five-yard touchdown of his own to reduce the deficit to just one. Brees then connected with McAllister on an 11-yard touchdown soon after. The Saints went up 27-21. The Superdome crowd went crazy.

After the Eagles scored on a fourth-quarter field goal, the Saints tried to milk the clock by running with the football exclusively. However, they fumbled after a pitchout play for running back Reggie Bush went awry. Philadelphia still had a chance.

The Eagles decided to punt on fourth down. Saints head coach Sean Payton told his team to run out the clock and run with the football on every play. When New Orleans got the first down inside the two-minute warning, the game was all but over–the Saints were headed to the 2006 NFC Championship Game against the Chicago Bears.

The Saints traveled to Chicago's Soldier Field for that particular game on January 21, 2007. The visiting team got off to a shaky start, committing two turnovers and falling behind 16-0 in the second quarter. A touchdown reception courtesy of Marques Colston prevented New Orleans from getting shut out in the first half.

The Saints continued to gain momentum. Brees threw a pass to Bush which resulted in an 88-yard touchdown. The Bears saw their lead dwindle to just two with a score of 16-14. For their part, New Orleans thought they could upset the NFC's No. 1 seed and play in Super Bowl XLI.

But it was not meant to be. The Bears scored 25 unanswered points to put the Saints away for good. Final score: Chicago 39, New Orleans 14.

Despite the loss, Brees and the Saints exceeded everybody's expectations. They won 10 games, earned the conference's No. 2 seed, and made it to the NFC title game. All of these occurred just a year after an awful 3-13 season in the wake of the nation's worst natural disaster in history.

After the loss to the Bears, Brees and his teammates arrived in New Orleans at 2 a.m. central time. Thousands of fans gathered at Louis Armstrong New Orleans International Airport to welcome them back home. "Who Dat?" had been the Saints' battle cry all season long. It was still very much the case on that day.

Brees was astonished. He could not believe how much the people of New Orleans loved their Saints. With an improved supporting cast and a loyal fan base, he knew the team would build on its success in 2007.

## 2007 NFL Season

Once the 2007 NFL season started, experts believed that the New Orleans Saints were no longer the "Aints" of old–a nickname their fans and critics had given them because of their tradition of losing year in and year out. Fortunately, they had turned a corner in 2006. They hoped they would be Super Bowl contenders for years to come. Drew Brees was an important part of that goal and had just come off his most successful season. If the San Diego Chargers and Miami Dolphins had doubted Brees' abilities as a starting quarterback in the NFL a few years ago, nobody doubted now—he was a bona fide star quarterback, and his second Pro Bowl berth proved it.

The Saints stumbled to a rough 0-4 start to the 2007 NFL season. They lost their season opener to the Indianapolis Colts in blowout fashion, 41-10, on September 6, 2007. They lost to the Tampa Bay Buccaneers, Tennessee Titans, and Carolina Panthers over their next three games. During New Orleans' four-game slide, they lost by an average of 17 points per contest. Brees was just a shadow of his old self, throwing for just one touchdown and nine interceptions during that losing streak.[xxxii] It was arguably the worst start of his NFL career.

However, the Saints managed to regroup. They won their next four games to even their win-loss record to 4-4 entering the Week 10 game against the St. Louis Rams. Brees played lights out during that four-game winning streak with 11 touchdowns and just 1 interception. New Orleans won by an average of almost 14 points during that span. One thing was clear: If Drew Brees played poorly, the New Orleans Saints were still the "Aints." If he played magnificently, the Saints were Super Bowl contenders.

Brees credited the turnaround to his teammate and wide receiver David Patten, per his autobiography. Patten told Brees that he had lost confidence. He had to become a better leader for his team. Brees took Patten's words to heart.

Brees' best game of the season was against the Jacksonville Jaguars in Week 9. He went 35-of-49 passing for 445 yards, 3 touchdowns, and no interceptions in the 41-24 victory.

"I'd say the swagger is back," Brees told the Associated Press (via ESPN). "We've got a good thing going…but by no means have we accomplished anything yet. That's something we need to realize."[xxxiii]

The Saints failed to build on their successful 2006 season. They went just 3-5 in their next eight games to finish with an overall win-loss record of 7-9. They could not overcome their slow start, and because of that, they missed the postseason yet again.

Drew Brees finished the season with 4,423 passing yards, 28 touchdowns, and 8 interceptions. Even if he managed to turn his game around, he was not able to lead his team to the playoffs. Brees and the Saints had to regroup for the following year.

## 2008 NFL Season

By now, Drew Brees was entering his eighth season in the National Football League and his third with New Orleans. He had two postseason appearances and two Pro Bowl berths to date. While these were good, nothing could ever compare to winning the Super Bowl. Brees and his teammates aimed high in 2008 after a disappointing campaign the year before.

The Saints turned out to be an average bunch in 2008. They would win one game and then lose the next and just could not gain any momentum.

Brees started the season strong with 343 yards, 3 touchdowns, and 1 interception in the Week 1 24-20 win over the Tampa Bay Buccaneers at home.[xxxiv] Hurricane Gustav made landfall in the days leading up to the Week 1 contest. The people of New Orleans were afraid it would be 2005 all over again. In his book, Brees said the Saints had to practice for the Buccaneers game at the Indianapolis Colts' new Lucas Oil Stadium while Hurricane Gustav battered New Orleans. He said that this hurricane did not reach Category 3 status, however, sparing the city from further damage.

"It was a great way to start the season off," Brees told the Associated Press (via ESPN). "Obviously, coming off a week where everyone was displaced from their homes here in New Orleans, and coming back and obviously having the fans back in full force–it was awesome."[xxxv]

The topsy-turvy nature of the season took full effect in the ensuing weeks for the Saints. They lost their next two games and then alternated wins and losses over the next five weeks. At that point, they had a 4-4 win-loss record entering their bye in Week 9.

Brees would have his best game of the season's second half against the Green Bay Packers in Week 12. He completed 20 of his 26 passes for 323 yards, 4 touchdowns, and no interceptions. The Saints led by just three points at the half, 24-21. However, they thoroughly outplayed the Packers in the last 30 minutes of the game. New Orleans outscored Green Bay 27-8, during that stretch. Saints running back Deuce McAllister set a franchise record with his 54th career touchdown in the victory.

"We're kind of in the middle of (the) pack, just like a lot of other teams," Brees commented after the game. "This is the time where a few of those teams start to separate themselves, and we want to be one of those teams."[xxxvi]

Brees and the Saints' best chance of accomplishing this was on the road against the Tampa Buccaneers the following week. Before that showdown, New Orleans had a 6-5 record. In the NFL, where teams played 16 games in the regular season, one win can make the difference. The Saints needed to win over the Buccaneers if they wanted to salvage their playoff hopes.

It was a 20-20 tie with less than four minutes left to play. The Saints had possession and a chance to march the ball downfield and kick a game-winning field goal. Instead, Brees threw a costly interception on the third play of the drive. The Buccaneers made a field goal on their side of the field on their ensuing possession. Brees threw another interception as time wound down, securing the heartbreaking loss.

In his autobiography, Brees said, "It was the worst I have ever felt after a game while wearing a Saints uniform." Nobody could blame him for feeling that way. The Saints fell to 6-6 on the season. They finished 2008 with a mediocre 8-8 record, missing the postseason for the second straight year. Brees threw for career bests of 5,069 yards and 34 touchdowns, but it all went for naught. He fell just 15 yards short of former Miami Dolphins quarterback Dan Marino's single-season passing yardage record (5,084 yards).

On the plus side, the Saints set several team records for scoring (461 points) and yards (6,751) in 2008, per Brees' autobiography.

New Orleans won 10 games and made it to the NFC Championship Game in 2006, but had been an average team since then. Would they reclaim their lost glory in 2009? Their fans held their breath in anticipation.

## 2009 NFL Season

Drew Brees was confident that his New Orleans Saints would put the past two seasons behind them and start on a clean slate in the 2009 NFL season. However, it would not be easy.

Even before the season kicked off, Brees experienced another personal tragedy. His mother Mina committed suicide on August 7, 2009. Brees found out about it when his wife Brittany showed up unexpectedly during a Saints closed practice at training camp. Brittany Brees received the sad news from her brother-in-law, Reid.

In his autobiography, Drew Brees said his mother visited a friend in Colorado, the same state where his brother lived. "She had packed prescription sleeping pills, pain pills, and antidepressants, some of which dated back to the 1990s," Brees said.

The autopsy results came out almost three months later. A November 21, 2009, report from the Associated Press (via

ESPN) confirmed Mina Brees' death as a suicide linked to substance abuse.[xxxvii] Drew Brees revealed that his mother was actually dealing with personal issues that affected her mental health.

During this tough time, Brees sought the advice of Godly people who were well-versed in Biblical scripture. In his words, "it was the most intense time of mourning I've ever experienced." Miraculously, he said the grief slowly dissipated as the 2009 NFL season was about to begin, per his autobiography. It was a season he would dedicate to his mother.

Brees started the season on a high note. He completed 26 of 34 passes for 358 yards, 6 touchdowns, and 1 interception in a 45-27 Week 1 win over the Detroit Lions.[xxxviii] Even though Detroit went winless in 16 games in 2008, the Saints were not about to take them lightly.

Better yet, this season-opening win set the tone for New Orleans. The team had been inconsistent for the last two seasons, to say the least. They would be a far cry from those Saints teams in 2008 and 2009.

They would also continue to play lights out on offense in their second game against the Philadelphia Eagles. The Saints were up by just four at halftime, 17-13. However, they would outscore the Eagles by 22 in the second half and go on to win, 48-22. Brees was extremely satisfied with how the offense clicked, per his autobiography. He said that they could not afford to get too excited just yet–the Saints' goal was Super Bowl XLIV or bust.

Brees looked forward to the Week 6 matchup against the New York Giants, who also sported an unblemished 5-0 record. It was a homecoming for the Giants' sixth-year quarterback, Eli Manning, who hails from New Orleans (his father Archie played for the Saints from 1971-82). It was his first NFL game in The Big Easy. Another intriguing storyline involved Saints tight end Jeremy Shockey, who was on the Giants' Super Bowl XLII-winning roster in 2007. New York traded him in 2008 and Brees was sure Shockey wanted a bit of payback.

New Orleans ran their record to 6-0 after the 48-27 win on October 18, 2009. The Saints scored 34 points in the first half and never looked back. Their offense had carried them yet again. Brees played magnificently, going 23-of-30 passing for 369 yards, 4 touchdowns, and no interceptions.

Early on, Brees had already thought about facing the Minnesota Vikings in the 2009 NFC Championship Game. Peyton Manning's Indianapolis Colts were also unbeaten at that point.

Brees envisioned the Saints going up against the Colts in Super Bowl XLIV in Miami, Florida.

"On the other side, in the AFC, we were watching the Colts go undefeated," he said in his autobiography. "They had some close games, but they were finishing them and winning. 'Get ready to face the Colts in the Super Bowl,' I thought. Every time something came on TV about the Colts, I looked at it like a boxer at a weigh-in, where you stand nose to nose. That's how I envisioned the season playing out. We were going to win home-field advantage, and the Vikings were coming to New Orleans. Then we would beat Indianapolis in Miami."

The Week 9 game against the Carolina Panthers on November 8, 2009, carried historical implications for the Saints. They had never gone 8-0 in franchise history. It was their chance to re-write the record books.

New Orleans was down 17-6 at the half. However, they fought back in the third quarter. Brees hit wide receiver Marques Colston for a 63-yard touchdown to trim the deficit to just four after the point after touchdown (PAT). After the Panthers scored a field goal, the Saints scored on another touchdown to even the score, 20-20.

New Orleans led for the first time after a successful field goal attempt in the fourth quarter. Several plays later, Saints defensive end Anthony Hargrove forced a fumble, recovered, and scored the insurance touchdown. Final score: New Orleans 30, Carolina 20. The Saints had gone 8-0 for the first time. Brees finished with 330 yards with 1 touchdown and 1 interception.

"That's great," Brees said. "I mean, 1967 until now and we're the only (Saints) team to have done that. That's really special. I feel like we've got a special group of guys, a special team, and certainly we're not satisfied with just being 8-0. We have what it takes to just continue to win."[xxxix]

Apparently, the Saints were just getting started. They won their next five games to go 13-0 on the season. Brees was superb, throwing for 15 touchdowns and just 3 interceptions during that 5-game stretch.

The Dallas Cowboys ended New Orleans' unbeaten run on December 19, 2009. They got off to a 24-3 lead after three quarters. The Saints managed to score two touchdowns in the fourth quarter, but it was not enough. Dallas prevailed, 24-17.

New Orleans also lost their last two games of the 2009 NFL season to the Tampa Bay Buccaneers and Carolina Panthers.

Saints head coach Sean Payton decided to sit out several of his key players (including Brees) in the season finale against Carolina to preserve their health for the postseason. Mark Brunell started in Brees' place in the season-ending 23-10 road loss to the Panthers on January 3, 2010.

The Saints finished with a 13-3 win-loss record in the 2009 NFL season. It was the best regular-season record in franchise history, eclipsing the previous team best of 12 wins of the 1992 New Orleans Saints.[xl]

New Orleans earned the No. 1 seed in the NFC and a first-round bye in the postseason.

For his part, Brees threw for 34 touchdowns for the second consecutive year. He also threw for 4,388 yards and 11 interceptions. He earned his second straight Pro Bowl nod, which was his third overall.

The Saints next set their sights on the Arizona Cardinals in the divisional round. The game took place at the Louisiana Superdome on January 16, 2010. The Cardinals struck first with a 70-yard touchdown from running back Tim Hightower. Saints running back Lynell Hamilton countered with a goal of his own to tie things up, 7-7. New Orleans then forced a fumble on the ensuing Arizona drive. Saints safety Darren Sharper scooped up the live ball and took it to the Cardinals' 37-yard line. Several plays later, Brees threw a pass to tight end Jeremy Shockey in the end zone and the Saints did not look back after that.

Their starting running back, Reggie Bush, scored a 46-yard touchdown and an 83-yard touchdown on a punt return. All in all, New Orleans scored on five of their six possessions in the first half to put the game out of reach. The Saints prevailed in a blow out with a score of 45-14. Brees finished with 247 yards, 3 touchdowns, and no interceptions.

Next up were the Minnesota Vikings in the 2009 NFC Championship Game on January 24, 2010. Brees' prediction near the midway point of the season came true. The Saints would face the Vikings for the right to represent their conference in Super Bowl XLIV in Miami.

Brees was used to facing Brett Favre, one of the greatest quarterbacks in the league. After spending the 2008 NFL season with the New York Jets, Favre signed with the Vikings, the Packers' NFC North nemesis, in summer of 2009, but he was already nearing the end of what was an all-time great career. The Saints also had to clamp down on the Vikings' two other weapons, wide receiver Sidney Rice and running back Adrian Peterson.

Peterson got things going with a touchdown in the first quarter. The Saints retaliated with a 38-yard touchdown from running back Pierre Thomas. No team had scored against Minnesota on its first drive of the game in 2009 until that Thomas touchdown, per Brees' autobiography. The Saints' quarterback saw it as a sign of good things to come.

Rice and Devery Henderson–two outstanding wide receivers–traded touchdowns to tie the score at 14-14. New Orleans special teamer Courtney Roby opened the second half with a 61-yard kickoff return, giving the Saints good field position. Thomas scored a touchdown to give New Orleans its first lead of the game. However, it was short-lived as Peterson countered with a goal.

The Saints recovered a Vikings fumble early in the fourth quarter. Brees then threw a pass to running back Reggie Bush, who officials thought ran just short of the end zone. On further review, they overturned the call to make it 28-21 for New Orleans. Peterson remained undaunted. He scored his third touchdown with five minutes left to play to tie things up yet again.

After the Saints came up empty in their next drive, the Vikings marched the ball downfield. On third and 15 with around 20 seconds left, Minnesota needed a completion to put it in field goal range. Instead, Favre threw an interception to Saints cornerback Tracy Porter to send the game into overtime.

New Orleans won the coin toss to start the extra session. On fourth down, the Vikings stopped the Saints just inches short of the former's 42-yard line. Saints head coach Sean Payton decided to go for it on fourth and inches. The gamble paid off and running back Pierre Thomas leaped over the line for the first down. Brees calmly led New Orleans to Minnesota's 32-yard line, setting up a possible game-winning field goal from Garrett Hartley. Hartley's kick sailed right through the uprights and the New Orleans Saints beat the Minnesota Vikings, 31-28.

It was no longer a dream. The Saints would move on to play in their first Super Bowl game. Drew Brees and his teammates were ecstatic and the home crowd went wild.

At the end of the game, Brees paid tribute to Favre. He said that it was an honor to be on the same field with one of the greatest players to ever play the game. Such an experience was something he personally treasured, especially in such a setting with the stakes as high as they were.

Brees would soon share the field with another great quarterback–the Indianapolis Colts' Peyton Manning–during

Super Bowl XLIV. The other part of his mid-season vision had come true. It would be a Saints vs. Colts showdown for the 45th edition of the Vince Lombardi Trophy.

## Super Bowl XLIV vs. Indianapolis Colts

The New Orleans Saints faced the Indianapolis Colts in Super Bowl XLIV at Sun Life Stadium in Miami, Florida on February 7, 2010. The two teams were the NFL's best throughout the course of the 2009 NFL season. It seemed inevitable that they would square off in the biggest game of the season. The Saints were gunning for their first title. On the other hand, the Colts were aiming for their second Super Bowl crown in four years (they beat the Chicago Bears in Super Bowl XLI, which was also in Miami).

Drew Brees wanted absolutely no distractions before the Super Bowl. In his autobiography, he said that the National Football League's requirements (such as an hour's worth of media daily before the Super Bowl) could have easily thrown him and his teammates off. Brees had always been meticulous about his preparation. He trained at the gym, watched films, practiced visualization, and took to the field for practice before a big game. The league's requirements could have distracted him. Nonetheless, the Saints were professionals, so they had to comply. "Don't see it as a chore," Super Bowl XXXIV-winning quarterback Kurt Warner told Brees. "Just embrace it."

Brees also admitted that he felt nervous before the game. A good number of the Colts' players were on the Super Bowl XLI-winning roster. In contrast, most of the Saints had never been to the Super Bowl. In the end, Brees and his teammates eased up and considered it for what it was–a hard-nosed football game.

Indianapolis struck first with a first-quarter field goal, forcing New Orleans to punt on the ensuing drive. Colts quarterback Peyton Manning capitalized, just as he had always done in his brilliant 13-year career. He threw a touchdown pass to wide receiver Pierre Garçon for an early 10-0 lead. Brees knew that being down by two scores to the Colts was not the ideal situation. The Saints had to fight back.

After they got on the board with a field goal, their defense forced Indianapolis to punt. When the Saints got the ball back, they marched the ball to the Colts' three-yard line. Unfortunately, Indianapolis' defense held and forced New Orleans into a fourth-and-goal situation. Saints head coach Sean Payton decided to go for the touchdown. Once again, the Colts stopped the Saints from reaching the end zone, leaving Brees and his teammates frustrated.

Nonetheless, New Orleans managed to get the ball back in the waning moments of the second quarter. After Brees had orchestrated a drive that put the Saints in field goal range, kicker Garrett Hartley added three more points to cut the deficit to four, 10-6.

Payton made another gutsy call, deciding to go for the onside kick at the beginning of the second half. The Saints did, recovered the football, and got possession. The gamble paid off. Several plays later, New Orleans executed a screen pass play for running back Pierre Thomas. He did the rest, scoring a touchdown to put the Saints up 13-10. Saints fans were delirious.

Not so fast. The Colts answered with a goal of their own to reclaim the lead. The Saints came right back with a field goal to put them within a point, 17-16.

Indianapolis seemed to gain momentum after converting on fourth-and-2 from New Orleans' 46-yard line. However, the Colts could not move the ball for a first down. Their kicker, Adam Vinatieri, missed a 51-yard field goal attempt which put the Saints in good field position.

The Saints relied on a combination of run and pass plays to move the ball to the Colts' two-yard line. Brees found tight end Jeremy Shockey running a slant route. Touchdown.

Sean Payton decided to go for the two-point conversion. Brees threw a sprint-out pass to wide receiver Lance Moore. Colts cornerback Jacob Lacey kicked the ball as soon as Moore caught it in the end zone. The officials ruled it an incompletion. Brees asked Moore if he caught the pass, and he replied in the affirmative. Brees then told Payton, who threw the challenge flag. Moments later, the officials overturned the call, saying that the two-point conversion was successful. Saints 24, Colts 17.

With time down to 5:35, Brees knew that Manning could still lead Indianapolis to a game-tying drive. The former even ran two-minute formation plays in his mind while the Colts had possession, per his autobiography.

Indianapolis had the ball on third-and-5 with around three minutes remaining. As it turned out, Manning threw an interception to Saints cornerback Tracy Porter, who ran the ball into the end zone for a pick-six. Lightning had struck twice. Porter picked off Brett Favre to preserve the tie in regulation during the NFC Championship Game. Now, he had intercepted the great Peyton Manning in Super Bowl XLIV. Indianapolis managed to move the ball to New Orleans' five-yard line. However, the Saints' defense stopped the Colts on fourth down with 44 seconds left.

Final score: New Orleans Saints 31, Indianapolis Colts 17. The Saints were the Super Bowl XLIV champions–their first title in their 42-year existence. Nine years after Drew Christopher Brees had stared down at Kansas City Chiefs head coach Dick Vermeil's Super Bowl ring during an interview at the 2001 NFL Scouting Combine, he had finally won his first Vince Lombardi Trophy.

Brees enjoyed every moment of it–he took in the applause of the Saints faithful in Miami and hugged all of his linemen after the game. Brees may have earned Super Bowl XLIV honors with his 288-yard, 2 touchdown performance, but he said that he would have never made the plays had his offensive line crumbled, per his autobiography. As it turned out, his O-line allowed just one sack in the Super Bowl, and the Saints quarterback made it clear that the victory was a complete team effort.

After New Orleans had made it to the 2006 NFC Championship Game against the Chicago Bears, they struggled through two mediocre seasons before winning the Super Bowl. Sometimes, one has to take two steps backward before they take a step forward. The Saints epitomized that in the 2009 NFL season.

For his part, Brees managed to overcome adversity. His mother had passed away during Saints training camp a little over five months before the Super Bowl. It was one of the toughest moments in his life. And yet, he persevered. His reward was that he had helped the city of New Orleans win their first Vince Lombardi Trophy.

Drew Brees finally uttered the line he had wanted to say since he started playing flag football at St. Andrew's Episcopal School during a post-game interview.

He said, "I'm going to Disney World!"

## 2010 NFL Season

Drew Brees had finally accomplished his dream of winning a Super Bowl. After years of futility, the New Orleans Saints were world champions. The bigger question loomed: Would they be able to win another title in 2010?

The first test came in Week 1 in a rematch against the Minnesota Vikings, the Saints' NFC Championship Game adversaries of the previous season. In that prior game, New Orleans cornerback Tracy Porter intercepted Minnesota quarterback Brett Favre in the waning seconds to force overtime. The Saints won on a Garrett Hartley field goal in the extra session.

The trend continued in 2010. The Saints still had Favre's number. Favre, who had been coming off offseason ankle surgery, could not get in a groove all game long. He threw for 171 yards, 1 touchdown, and 1 interception, but Minnesota scored just 9 points—all in the first half. The Vikings held on to a 9-7 lead after the first 30 minutes, but could not sustain their momentum. New Orleans also held Pro Bowl running back Adrian Peterson to just 87 yards on 19 carries. He had had 3 touchdowns and 122 yards in the 2009 NFC Championship Game against the Saints.

As for Brees, he got off to an excellent start in the 2010 NFL season. He and his teammates enjoyed the pre-game festivities. Singer and New Orleans native Harry Connick, Jr. rode a float with Saints owner Tom Benson, who held the Vince Lombardi Trophy. Saints game-day staff unfurled the team's 2009 Super Bowl Championship banner as Connick sang "When the Saints Go Marching In." The Saints then marched out of the tunnel to the thunderous ovation of the Louisiana Superdome crowd. Brees stood on the 30-yard line moments before kickoff and led the crowd in chants of, "Who dat say dey gonna beat dem Saints!"

Brees' touchdown strike to Devery Henderson on the fifth play of the game set the tone. Running back Pierre Thomas added another touchdown for New Orleans in the third quarter. According to ESPN, it was "the lowest-scoring victory of the Sean Payton era."[xli] It was not pretty, but Brees and his teammates took it.

The Saints were inconsistent in their next six games, alternating wins and losses during the stretch. Brees' best performance was in a 31-6 win over the Tampa Bay Buccaneers in Week 6. He went 21-of-32 passing for 263 yards, 3 touchdowns, and 1 interception.[xlii]

Brees followed that up with his worst game of the season. Despite throwing for 356 yards and 2 touchdowns, he also threw 4 interceptions in an embarrassing 30-17 loss to the Cleveland Browns, a team that won just five games in 2009, at home. Brees threw two pick-sixes (an interception returned for a touchdown) to 33-year-old Cleveland linebacker David Bowens.

"Whenever you throw a pick, you're going to be upset," Brees told ESPN. "Four interceptions are hard to swallow. I think we are all doing a little soul searching. We know how good we can be. Obviously, we aren't playing that way right now."[xliii]

Brees was correct. New Orleans had to do some serious soul searching. The loss dropped the Saints to 4-3 on the season. Other teams would have been satisfied, but it was not close to good enough for the defending Super Bowl champions.

The loss to the Browns seemed to have fired the Saints up. New Orleans went on a six-game winning streak, beating the opposition by an average of 13.1 points per game. Brees recorded 14 touchdown passes and 8 interceptions during that run. The Saints cooled off during the season's home stretch, losing two of their last three games to finish with an 11-5 win-loss record. Brees wound up with 4,620 yards, 33 touchdowns, and 22 interceptions in 2010. He earned his third straight Pro Bowl nod and fifth overall.

Despite winning 11 games, the New Orleans Saints were only the No. 5 seed in the NFC. They would face the fourth-seeded Seattle Seahawks on the road in the 2010 Wild Card round.

Despite winning just 7 of their 16 regular-season games in 2010, the Seahawks won their division. The NFC West was terrible that year. No team had a winning record. Seattle won the tiebreaker over the St. Louis Rams (7-9). The San Francisco

49ers and Arizona Cardinals won six and five games, respectively.<sup>xliv</sup>

On paper, it seemed the Saints–the defending Super Bowl champions and 10-point favorites–would roll over the Seahawks. On the day of their NFC Wild Card Game on January 8, 2011, this proved to be an inaccurate assumption.

The Saints led 10-0 after a Garrett Hartley field goal and Heath Evans touchdown. The Seahawks countered with a John Carlson goal to inch within 10-7. New Orleans regained the lead in the second quarter after running back Julius Jones scored on a five-yard touchdown run. Less than three minutes later, Carlson scored his second goal to make it 17-14 for New Orleans after the point after touchdown. Olindo Mare's 29-yard field goal tied things up four minutes later.

The Seahawks then went on a nine-play, 76-yard drive which ended in a Brandon Stokley touchdown with 1:15 to go in the second quarter. It was Seattle quarterback Matt Hasselbeck's third touchdown pass of the first half. Brees managed to lead the Saints 77 yards downfield on their ensuing series. Hartley's second field goal made it 24-20 for Seattle at halftime.

Surprisingly, Seattle pulled away in the third quarter. Hasselbeck threw his fourth touchdown pass of the game at the

11:55 mark. This time, it was wide receiver Mike Williams who caught the ball. Mare added his second field goal of the game six-and-a-half minutes later for a commanding 34-20 lead at the end of the third quarter.

New Orleans mounted a comeback in the fourth quarter. Jones scored his second touchdown, and Hartley added his second field goal to make it 34-30 for Seattle.

It set the stage for Seahawks running back Marshawn Lynch. Nicknamed "Beast Mode," Lynch showed the Saints why he was one of the NFL's top running backs. On second down on Seattle's 33-yard line and with a little over four minutes left, Lynch took the handoff from Hasselbeck. He broke six tackles as he made his way into the end zone. The Seahawks fans, known collectively as "The 12th Man," erupted. It was so loud at Qwest Field (later known as CenturyLink Field) that the ground shook after Lynch's touchdown. That scoring play aptly earned the nickname "The Beast Quake."

Nonetheless, the Saints fought back. Brees found Devery Henderson in the end zone with 1:34 left. New Orleans fullback DeShawn Wynn tried to get into the end zone for the two-point conversion, but the Seattle defense stopped him. The Seahawks ran out the clock and won 41-36.[xlv]

Brees played his guts out, throwing for 404 yards, 2 touchdowns, and no interceptions. The difference turned out to be New Orleans' lack of production on the ground. The Seahawks outgained the Saints, 150 yards to 77. Lynch accounted for 131 of his team's rushing yards, and in contrast, Saints running back Reggie Bush had just 12 yards on 5 carries. The Seattle Seahawks advanced to the NFC Divisional Round against the Chicago Bears. The New Orleans Saints were not able to defend their Super Bowl title. They were going home.

Drew Brees had been a top-tier quarterback for the Saints since he signed with them in 2005. Chances were that the trend would continue in 2011. He and his teammates hoped to put the Seattle loss behind them and start with a clean slate the following season.

## 2011 NFL Season

The New Orleans Saints' 2010 season ended on a sour note when they lost to the Seattle Seahawks in the NFC Wild Card Round. They also lost their grip on the Super Bowl crown.

New Orleans' goal was simple: They wanted to be Super Bowl champions again. To achieve this objective, they added the likes of wide receiver Lance Moore, linebacker Jo-Lonn Dunbar, and safety Roman Harper in the offseason.

However, even before Drew Brees and his teammates took the field in 2011, the NFL had to deal with a major issue in a lockout of its players.

The league formally announced the beginning of the work stoppage on March 12, 2011, after the 32 team owners and players (represented by the NFL Players Association) could not agree on a new collective bargaining agreement (CBA). Brees, New England Patriots quarterback Tom Brady, and Indianapolis Colts quarterback Peyton Manning filed antitrust lawsuits against the NFL in an attempt to prevent the lockout.[xlvi] The players eventually approved the settlement of their antitrust litigation on July 25, 2011, effectively ending the lockout.[xlvii]

Throughout that time, Brees played an active role. It was said that he was probably the most active player in that labor dispute because of how he was always there trying to negotiate on behalf of his fellow players. Nevertheless, his presence during the lockout earned him detractors all over the country as fans of football were only looking forward to watching games rather than to see their favorite players getting treated well by team ownership.[xlviii]

Brees might have been busy with his role in the lockout, but that did not stop him from preparing for the 2011 NFL season.

According to Sam Farmer of the Associated Press, Brees helped organize player-run training sessions at Tulane University in New Orleans for six months during the work stoppage. As a matter of fact, he even helped shoulder the fees for trainers, insurance, and accommodation for his teammates. The Saints quarterback thought about the idea even before the 2010 postseason ended. Even back then, he anticipated a lockout could be a reality. While the 2011 NFL season's fate hung in the balance, Brees thought the Saints should be ready for anything. The last thing he and the other veterans wanted was for the rookies to have minimal knowledge of their playbook. They could not have afforded to cram and make hasty, last-minute preparations if the dispute ended just before the season began.

Even though the Saints lost their Week 1 game to the Green Bay Packers, 42-34, they won their next four. Brees was off to a solid start, throwing for 1,769 yards and 12 touchdowns to help New Orleans to a 4-1 record.

Brees' most impressive performance of the season came on October 23, 2011. He threw for 325 yards, 5 touchdowns, and no interceptions in a 62-0 rout of the visiting Indianapolis Colts in Week 7. He threw two touchdowns each to wide receiver

Marques Colston and tight end Jimmy Graham. Running back Darren Sproles caught Brees' other touchdown pass.

The Colts were playing without starting quarterback Peyton Manning, who had undergone three neck surgeries over the past 19 months. Third-year quarterback Curtis Painter started in Manning's place, throwing for just 67 yards and an interception. With the loss, Indianapolis stumbled to its seventh loss in as many games. New Orleans won its fifth in seven.

After a 31-21 loss to the St. Louis Rams on the road in Week 8, the New Orleans Saints won eight consecutive games to finish the 2011 NFL season. It was reminiscent of the 13-3 team which had won the Super Bowl two seasons before. This version sported an identical record. Would it be déjà vu all over again?

The Week 16 game against the Atlanta Falcons on December 26, 2011, was the pinnacle of Drew Brees' regular season. He broke Dan Marino's single-season passing mark, throwing for 307 yards, 4 touchdowns, and 1 interception in the 45-16 blowout victory. As a result, Brees upped his season passing yardage to 5,169, beating Marino's old record of 5,084 yards. Brees' nine-yard pass to Sproles displaced Marino in the NFL record books.

More importantly, the win clinched the NFC South for the Saints.

To his credit, Drew Brees actually was not thinking about the record and was not aiming to break it. He knew that he had a chance to do so because there were a few people around him mentioning it. However, he focused more on the task at hand instead of on the record.[xlix]

Brees finished the 2011 NFL season with a career-high 46 touchdown passes. He added 5,476 passing yards and made it to the Pro Bowl for the fourth straight year and his sixth berth overall. It seemed those offseason workouts at Tulane University had paid off.

Despite winning the NFC South, the Saints were just the No. 3 seed in the NFC. That meant they had to play in the Wild Card Round against the sixth-seeded Detroit Lions.

Drew Brees managed to carry his regular-season magic into the postseason. He threw for 466 yards and 3 touchdowns in the 45-28 win over Detroit on January 7, 2012. Nobody could stop him.

The Lions led 14-10 at the half after quarterback Matthew Stafford threw touchdown passes to Will Heller and Calvin

Johnson. Brees took matters into his hands during the third quarter, throwing two touchdown passes to Devery Henderson and Jimmy Graham. New Orleans led, 23-14. Stafford's one-yard touchdown run made it 24-21 for the Saints after the successful point after touchdown conversion.

The Saints put the game away for good in the fourth quarter. Running back Darren Sproles scored on a 17-yard touchdown run with less than 10 minutes to go. Brees recorded his third touchdown pass two-and-a-half minutes later. Wide receiver Robert Meachem caught the football to give New Orleans a 38-21 lead. The Saints would never look back.

Brees said after the game that New Orleans needed to execute one play at a time to overcome the halftime deficit.[1] The Saints executed their game plan to perfection in the second half. They would advance to play the San Francisco 49ers in the Divisional Round.

San Francisco had been a mediocre team during the past decade, winning just two games in 2004. Their best record before the 2011 NFL season was an 8-8 showing in 2009. But in 2011, the 49ers won 13 games and the NFC West division. By doing so, they earned the No. 2 seed in their conference. Suffice it to say, San Francisco–arguably the team of the 1990s–had a recent history similar to New Orleans. The team was average at best but had winning seasons here and there. The 49ers and Saints were going to slug it out for the right to advance to the 2011 NFC Championship Game.

San Francisco seized control early in the game. Quarterback Alex Smith threw a 49-yard pass to tight end Vernon Davis on the second play of the match. With 44 seconds left in the first quarter, Smith struck again, throwing a four-yard pass to wide receiver Michael Crabtree to extend the 49ers' lead to 14-0. David Akers' 25-yard field goal in the opening moments of the second quarter made it 17-0 for San Francisco.

The Saints fought back. Brees recorded two touchdown passes in the second quarter, one to Jimmy Graham and the other to Marques Colston, to trim the deficit to just three at the half. A series of field goals in the third and fourth quarters made it 23-17 for the 49ers. Brees then connected with Darren Sproles on a 44-yard touchdown play. The Saints tasted their first lead of the game, 24-23, after John Kasay connected on his extra-point attempt.

Less than two minutes later, Smith, who thrived in first-year head coach Jim Harbaugh's system, ran for a 29-yard touchdown. However, running back Frank Gore's two-point conversion attempt failed. Brees threw his second touchdown pass to Graham–this one was good for 66 yards–with 1:48 left. Sproles then caught a pass from Brees for the two-point conversion to make it 32-29 for New Orleans.

However, there was still 1:37 left on the game clock, which was plenty of time for the 49ers to execute their hurry-up offense. The Saints' defense needed to pull out all the stops.

Alas, they could not.

On third-and-4 with just 14 seconds remaining, Smith somehow found Davis open down the middle. Davis did the rest and hauled it in for a 14-yard touchdown (he dubbed his touchdown "The Grab," a unique nickname similar to Dwight Clark's famous "The Catch" play in the 1981 NFC Championship Game).[li] San Francisco reclaimed the lead, 36-32. With nine seconds left, the Saints had practically no time to score a touchdown. The 49ers moved on. The Saints' season ended on a sad note yet again. Marshawn Lynch and Vernon Davis ending their title quests in consecutive years were tough pills to swallow.

New Orleans fell to 0-5 in road playoff games in its 44-year franchise history, per ESPN. Drew Brees and the Saints needed to regroup in the offseason and hope for a better postseason finish in the 2012 NFL season.

## 2012 NFL Season

Drew Christopher Brees has had his share of ups and downs–his parents' divorce, the freak shoulder injury he suffered against the San Diego Chargers in 2005, his mother's suicide, and several playoff disappointments, among other things. He and his teammates would encounter another obstacle before the 2012 NFL season even began.

NFL commissioner Roger Goodell decided to suspend the Saints' head coach Sean Payton and Gregg Williams, who was formerly their defensive coordinator (then with the St. Louis Rams), for their alleged involvement in the infamous Bountygate Scandal. Goodell suspended Payton for the whole season and suspended Williams indefinitely. The latter was eligible for reinstatement in 2013.[lii]

Goodell also suspended Saints general manager Mickey Loomis and the team's assistant, Joe Vitt, for eight and six games respectively. The NFL commissioner said that his investigators concluded that the team ran a bounty system where the players earned bonuses for hurting their opponents. They also said that Payton and Loomis knew about the system all along and even lied about it to the league. Payton and Loomis refused to listen to Saints owner Tom Benson and the NFL, who both tried to convince them to stop.

New Orleans tapped assistant head coach and linebacker coach Joe Vitt to be their interim coach for the 2012 NFL season.

"I am speechless," Brees wrote on Twitter (via *The New York Daily News*). "Sean Payton is a great man, coach, and mentor. The best there is. I need to hear an explanation for this punishment."

Despite the Bountygate scandal, he would savor another victory in 2012.

Brees signed a five-year, $100 million contract extension on July 15th. The deal included a $60 million guaranteed purse and a $37 million signing bonus, per NFL.com. He called the experience "surreal" because of how crazy the past offseason was and how he was only excited to get back to work and help his team win in the next season.[liii]

Brees also said he was excited to go against the schemes of new Saints defensive coordinator Steve Spagnuolo during training camp, per NFL.com.

Apparently, Spagnuolo's addition was not enough to offset the absence of Payton and Williams. The Saints got off to a horrible 0-4 start and lost by an average of just five points during that slide. Brees threw ten touchdowns and five interceptions. New Orleans beat his former team, the San Diego Chargers, in Week 5 to improve to 1-4 heading into its bye week.[liv]

The Saints hit their stride in their next five games, going 4-1 after they beat the Oakland Raiders, 38-17, in Week 11. Brees threw for 14 touchdowns and just 3 interceptions during that five-game run, per NFL.com. New Orleans won their third straight game and evened their record to 5-5 on the season.

Brees, who passed for 219 yards and 3 touchdowns in the crucial road game against the Raiders, could not have been more relieved as the New Orleans Saints were staying the course after overcoming such a rough start. They were able to turn things for the better, which was something that fans and critics thought was unrealistic.[lv]

Unfortunately, New Orleans could not build on their three-game winning streak. They lost three consecutive games to the San Francisco 49ers, Atlanta Falcons, and New York Giants to fall out of playoff contention. The Saints did win two of their last three games. However, it was too late. Their 7-9 record put them in a three-way tie for second place in the NFC South behind the 13-3 Atlanta Falcons. It was New Orleans' first time to miss the postseason in four years and the team's first losing record since 2012. Brees put up great numbers (5,177 yards and 43 touchdowns), but they went for naught.

He passed for four touchdowns in the season-ending 44-38 home loss to the Carolina Panthers on December 30th. Brees became the first player in NFL history to record 5,000 yards in a season three times. He also made it to the Pro Bowl for the fifth straight year (seventh overall selection). His head coach, Sean Payton, whose year-long suspension ended after Super Bowl XLVII (which the city of New Orleans hosted) on February 3, 2013, recently agreed to a five-year contract extension.

Brees was very disappointed with how the Saints 2012 NFL season had turned out. However, for him, it served as an eye-opener that they were not playing up to their standards as a team. Luckily for them, they were going to get their head coach back the following season and were ready to get rolling after such a bad season.[lvi]

With Payton back in 2013, there was nowhere for the New Orleans Saints to go but up.

## 2013 NFL Season

The New Orleans Saints had endured a rough 2012 NFL season. They finished with a 7-9 win-loss record and missed the playoffs, but they were confident they would turn things around with the return of head coach Sean Payton.

For his part, Brees refused to blame interim coach Joe Vitt and his staff for the Saints' shortcomings the season before. He told *USA Today Sports'* Erik Brady on September 4, 2013, that "last season's staff coached well" but wished "our record reflected that." Payton's return served as a boost of confidence for the seven-time Pro Bowl quarterback, who gave credit to his head coach for believing in him, even when he had doubts about himself.[lvii]

The Saints opened the 2013 NFL season against their NFC South nemesis, the Atlanta Falcons, on September 8th. Seven years before, the Saints and Falcons tussled in the Louisiana Superdome–the first regular-season game in New Orleans since Hurricane Katrina devastated the city on August 30, 2005. The two squads' Week 1 game in 2013 also carried historical implications: Sean Payton's return after a one-year suspension due to the Bountygate scandal.

On this day, Brees and the Saints did not disappoint.

The New Orleans quarterback recorded 357 passing yards and 2 touchdowns in the 23-17 win over Atlanta. Welcome back, Sean Payton.

One of the Saints head coach's objectives was to shore up his team's matador defense, which yielded a single-season record of 7,042 yards in 2012, per ESPN. Payton hired former Dallas Cowboys defensive coordinator Rob Ryan (twin brother of then-New York Jets head coach Rex Ryan) to fix the problem. The Week 1 game against the Falcons was the first time a Sean Payton-coached team elected to defend after it won the opening coin toss–a sure sign he trusted Ryan's new defensive scheme. The Saints' new defense also impressed Brees from start to finish.[lviii]

Payton's return coupled with a new defense gave New Orleans a new lease on life, and the Saints won their first five games of the season. It seemed as if it was their Super Bowl-winning 2009 season all over again. Brees recorded 12 touchdowns and 4 interceptions during the winning streak.[lix] The Saints dropped a 30-27 heartbreaker to the New England Patriots in Week 6. They were 5-1 heading into their bye week.

New Orleans promptly won four of their next five games. The Saints' most impressive showing to date was their back-to-back wins over the Dallas Cowboys (49-17) and San Francisco 49ers (23-20) in Weeks 11 and 12. Brees threw for 392 yards, 4 touchdowns, and no interceptions in the win over Dallas. He had 305 passing yards, 1 touchdown, and 1 interception in the triumph over San Francisco.

In that game, Brees fumbled with 3:12 remaining. However, 49ers linebacker Ahmad Brooks drew a late-hit penalty after he clotheslined Brees just as he let go of the football. The hit bloodied Brees' chin and also resulted in a late Garrett Hartley field goal to help the Saints beat the 49ers. New Orleans improved to 8-2 on the season despite recording three turnovers. San Francisco dropped to 6-4.

"You're going to have games like this," Brees told ESPN afterward. "You still find ways to win against a playoff-caliber opponent with a lot at stake at this point in the season. That says a lot."[lx]

The Saints now controlled their destinies. They were in a fierce battle with the Carolina Panthers for NFC South supremacy. Alas, New Orleans lost three of their last five games to finish 11-5 on the season. They also lost their grip on the division title and a first-round playoff bye as the Panthers wound up with a

12-4 win-loss record. Brees had 11 touchdowns and 4 interceptions in the Saints' late-season slide, per NFL.com.

The Saints were in a precarious situation leading up to the Week 17 finale against the Tampa Bay Buccaneers. They had lost three of their previous four games and were in danger of missing the postseason. The Saints put their fans' fears to rest, however, with a resounding 42-17 win at home to clinch a spot in the Wild Card Round against the Philadelphia Eagles.

Brees, who completed 24 of his 31 pass attempts for 381 yards, 4 touchdowns, and no interceptions, told ESPN that Payton's return was a huge factor in New Orleans' return to the postseason.

"Obviously, Sean's a huge part of the Saints' return to the playoffs," he said. "Four out of five years, winning an average of 12 games in every one of those (playoff) years. That's a big deal."[lxi]

Brees finished the 2013 NFL season with his fourth 5,000-yard effort. To be more precise, he had 5,162 yards, 39 touchdowns, and 12 interceptions. He earned yet another Pro Bowl nod–his sixth consecutive and eighth overall.

Payton's hiring of Rob Ryan was a huge factor in New Orleans' turnaround–the Saints were just one of four teams that surrendered fewer than five thousand yards to their opponents in 2013. New Orleans gave up just 4,891 yards, ranking the team fourth in overall defense.[lxii]

Going into the playoffs, the Saints were hoping their defense could shut down the Philadelphia Eagles, a team that had the second-best offense (6,676 total yards) in the entire league.[lxiii]

New Orleans took on Philadelphia in the 2013 NFC Wild Card Game at the latter's Lincoln Financial Field on January 4, 2014. After a scoreless first quarter, the Saints struck first with a 36-yard Shayne Graham field goal midway through the second quarter. Brees had a chance to strike again with 5:43 left in the second quarter, however, on first-and-10 at the Eagles' 49-yard line, he threw an interception to Philadelphia cornerback Bradley Fletcher. Several plays later, Saints kicker Shayne Graham followed up with another Saints field goal at the end of the quarter—but not before the Eagles scored a touchdown to lead the game 7-6 at the half. The Saints surged to retake the lead with two touchdowns in the third quarter, but the Eagles battled back once again to lead by a single point in the fourth quarter, 24-23.

The game was fought as hard as any could be and it came right down to a drive that required all of Drew Brees' veteran instincts and superior decision-making skills.

There was 4:35 left in the match. Brees, by now a 13-year veteran, calmly orchestrated a 10-play, 35-yard drive that milked almost the entire game clock. It set up a 32-yard, game-winning field goal attempt from Graham with just three seconds left. And Graham did not disappoint. His field goal sailed right through the uprights and the Saints won the Wild Card match by two points.

New Orleans finally shook off their past playoff ghosts. The Saints were marching on to the 2013 NFC Divisional Round against the very same team that beat them three seasons before, the Seattle Seahawks. They finally recorded the first playoff victory on the road in franchise history after a span of almost 47 years.

Unfortunately for the New Orleans Saints, an improved Seattle Seahawks team was more than a match for them in the next game. Unlike the last time they met in the playoffs, the Saints were now the underdogs. Meanwhile, the Seahawks were legit title contenders. Seattle defeated the Saints 23-15 in that round and would go on to eventually win Super Bowl XLVIII against the Denver Broncos.

A dejected Brees, who completed 24 of 43 passes for 309 yards and 1 touchdown, spoke about the Saints' inability to make the most of their playoff opportunities.

"You just don't know how many opportunities you're going to have," he told ESPN. "That's what makes it so tough standing up here and talking about it."[lxiv]

When New Orleans lost to Seattle in the 2013 NFC Divisional Round, Drew Brees was just four days shy of his 35th birthday. He was not getting any younger. Would he be able to revive the Saints' flickering playoff hopes in 2014?

## 2014 NFL Season

The 2014 NFL season would prove to be a challenging one for Drew Brees and his New Orleans Saints.

They lost their first two games by game-winning field goals to the Atlanta Falcons and Cleveland Browns. Losing to the Browns—a bonafide lottery team—was especially painful. Quarterback Brian Hoyer led Cleveland on a late 85-yard drive to set up Billy Cundiff's game-winning 29-yard field goal.

Despite the loss, Brees moved into the NFL history record books once again. He threw two touchdown passes to tight end Jimmy Graham. It moved him to fourth on the league's all-time career yardage list. Brees, who completed 27 of 40 pass attempts for 237 yards, overtook Denver Broncos Hall-of-Fame quarterback John Elway.

But personal records did nothing to ease his dissatisfaction. Brees had ended the previous season in disappointment and he felt the same way after the Week 2 loss to the Browns.

"It's frustrating because we expect to win," he commented afterward. "You can point to one play in each of these games. We're one play away in each of these games from being 2-0 instead of 0-2. That hurts."[lxv]

The Saints finally broke into the win column with a 20-9 triumph over the Minnesota Vikings in Week 3. New Orleans won two of their three games heading into their Week 6 bye to improve to 2-3. Brees had nine touchdowns and five interceptions during that stretch.

The bye week often helps a team regroup and focus for the grind that lies ahead. But it was not that way at all for New Orleans in 2014.

The Saints went on to lose four of their next six games. They lost by an average of seven points to powerhouses such as the Green Bay Packers, Cincinnati Bengals, and Baltimore Ravens. Brees did all he could, recording 13 touchdowns with just 5 interceptions during the slide. However, New Orleans had a 4-7 win-loss record through Week 12. Their playoff hopes were in serious jeopardy.

Brees earned another accolade in the 24-23 loss to the Detroit Lions in Week 7 by overtaking Chad Pennington's record to become the NFL's all-time most accurate passer. [lxvi] He completed 28 of 45 passes for 342 yards, 2 touchdowns, and 1 interception against Detroit, upping his career completion percentage to 66.21 percent.

Brees did not express his sentiments about the achievement after the heart-breaking defeat. The Saints had a 23-10 lead with just 3:38 remaining in the game before surrendering two late touchdowns. Brees threw an interception to Lions safety Glover Quin to seal the outcome in the fourth quarter.

The Saints' frustrations grew as the season wore on. Nonetheless, Brees continued re-writing the record books. He recorded his 30th touchdown pass of the 2014 NFL season in a 31-15 win over the Chicago Bears on December 15th.

According to *The New Orleans Times-Picayune's* Katherine Terrell, Brees extended his streak to seven consecutive seasons. Not only that, but Brees also threw at least 4,000 yards for a record ninth straight time.[lxvii]

New Orleans won three of their last five games to finish the season at 7-9 and dropped out of playoff contention. The Saints had averaged 11 wins over the past five seasons, a far cry from their past performances.

Brees poured out his emotions in an interview on January 26, 2015, with MMQB editor-in-chief Peter King.

"It was my most frustrating season," Brees said after the Pro Bowl Game. "You never want to go 7-9. It's no fun."[lxviii]

He finished with 4,952 yards, 33 touchdowns, and 17 interceptions.[lxix] It was his first time in four seasons not to surpass the 5,000-yard mark.

Brees was already 36 years old. His goal of winning another Super Bowl ring was slipping away. His assortment of records in the 2014 NFL season proved that he could play at the game's highest level, but would he ever have that opportunity again? Brees hoped the Saints could put the dismal year behind them and start with a clean slate in 2015.

## 2015 NFL Season

Drew Brees had suffered through a disappointing 7-9 season in 2014. He may have been older, but he could still play with the best of them. Look no further than the likes of Roger Staubach, Jim Plunkett, Kurt Warner, and John Elway. Staubach was 35 years old when his Dallas Cowboys defeated the Denver Broncos, 27-10, in Super Bowl XII. Plunkett was Brees' age when he led the Raiders to a 38-9 rout of the Washington Redskins in Super Bowl XVIII. A 37-year-old Warner steered the Rams to victory in Super Bowl XXXIV. Finally, John Elway was 37 and 38 years old when his Denver Broncos won Super Bowl XXXII and Super Bowl XXXIII.[lxx]

Should Brees and the New Orleans Saints win Super Bowl XLIX, he would be in good company.

The 2015 season got off to a rough start. The ghosts of 2014 seemed to haunt the New Orleans Saints–they lost their first three games. Observers noticed Brees loosening his right shoulder in the Week 2 loss to the visiting Tampa Bay Buccaneers because of a first-half hit that he took. He told ESPN after the game that he was not concerned about it and never considered taking himself out.[lxxi]

However, CBS Sports' Will Brinson reported on September 25, 2015, that Brees would sit out the Week 3 game against the Carolina Panthers due to that shoulder injury. His backup, Luke McCown, would take over the starting quarterback chores.[lxxii] He filled in admirably, completing 31 of 38 pass attempts for 310 yards, but it was not enough to overcome the team's 27-22 loss.

When Brees returned on October 4th against the Dallas Cowboys, he led New Orleans to their first win of the 2015 NFL season. His short pass to running back C.J. Spiller in overtime resulted in the 26-20 victory. Spiller broke loose for 80 yards on the game-winning play. It was the fastest regular-season overtime win in league history, per *USA Today's* Chris Chase.[lxxiii]

Brees completed 33 of 41 passes for 359 yards and 2 touchdowns. In doing so, he became just the fifth quarterback in NFL history to throw for 400 touchdowns. According to ESPN, he did it the fastest, accomplishing the feat in just 205 games. Not only that, but he also recorded his 5,000th career pass when he found tight end Josh Hill in the end zone with 3:48 remaining in the first quarter. Once the game concluded, Brees told ESPN that his shoulder "felt good enough."[lxxiv]

It was the kind of news that the Saints needed to hear. Brees promptly led New Orleans to a 3-1 record in their next four games. He threw for 11 touchdowns and 4 interceptions during that span.

The 36-year-old Brees continued to re-write NFL history books as the season wore on. He threw for a career-high 7 touchdowns in an exciting 52-49 win over the New York Giants on November 1st. He completed 39 of 50 passes for 505 yards and 2 interceptions. His counterpart, Giants quarterback Eli Manning, also had a great game with 30-of-41 passing for 350 yards, six touchdowns, and no interceptions. Brees and Manning combined for a record number of passing touchdowns in an NFL regular-season game. Brees also became only the eighth NFL player to throw for seven touchdowns in a match.[lxxv] Brees' predecessors were Sid Luckman, Adrian Burk, George Blanda, Y.A. Tittle, Joe Kapp, Peyton Manning, and Nick Foles.

The Saints and Giants combined for 101 points and 1,030 yards in the Week 8 shootout. According to ESPN, their combined score is the third-highest in NFL history.[lxxvi]

"Never been a part of something like that," Brees told the network afterward. "Pretty wild."

The game against the Giants turned out to be the main highlight of the Saints' disappointing season. New Orleans went on a four-game losing streak after the win over New York. Brees and his teammates were an inconsistent bunch, scoring 28, 14, 6, and 38 points during that slide, which dropped them to 4-8 overall.

The Saints' quarterback was not as productive. Usually, Brees would throw at least 12 touchdowns in 4 games, but he recorded just 8 points during the losing streak. The Houston Texans even shut him out completely in their Week 12 game on November 29, 2015. They held him without a touchdown pass. He even threw an interception in the 24-6 loss at Reliant Stadium in Houston, Texas. It was the first time in a decade, after a streak of 155 games, that New Orleans failed to score a touchdown in a game. It was also Brees' first time not to throw for a touchdown in 46 games, a testament to the stingy Texans' defense.[lxxvii]

New Orleans rebounded a bit to win three of their last four games of the 2015 NFL season, finishing with a 7-9 win-loss record. The Saints finished third in the NFC South and missed the postseason for the second consecutive year. They also failed to advance to the playoffs for the third time in four seasons. Nonetheless, Brees set several more records, becoming just the fourth quarterback to pass for 60,000 yards in a career when he threw for 341 yards and 3 touchdowns in a 35-27 Week 15 loss to the Detroit Lions at home. He also recorded his 10th straight 4,000-yard season.[lxxviii] Even though he injured his right foot in the second quarter, he did not miss a snap.

He played through pain in the Saints' next game, a 38-27 triumph over the visiting Jacksonville Jaguars at the Louisiana Superdome on December 27, 2015. Brees went 25-of-36 passing for 412 yards and 3 touchdowns with no interceptions. This increased his touchdown pass total to 31 for the season, extending his NFL-record eighth consecutive season with at least 31 touchdown passes.

Instead of talking about his records, Brees told ESPN that the win over Jacksonville was something New Orleans could build on for the foreseeable future.

"People might say we have nothing to play for as far as playoffs and such, but we have a lot to play for," he said. "We're continuing to build what is going to be a great team for years to come."[lxxix]

Brees threw for 4,870 yards, 32 touchdowns, and 11 interceptions in 2015. Despite his advancing age, he proved that he can still compete with the best of them. It was just unfortunate he did not have a stellar supporting cast the past two years. If Saints' management could acquire better players with Drew Brees as the quarterback, New Orleans should find itself in playoff contention sooner than later.

## 2016 Season

Going into the 2016 season, Drew Brees had never missed the playoffs in three straight years since arriving in New Orleans in 2016. The Saints expected to be chasing the Carolina Panthers, who lost in the Super Bowl to the Denver Broncos but still maintained the nucleus of a team that went 15-1 in 2015. Additionally, the Atlanta Falcons were on the upswing, as were the Tampa Bay Buccaneers, who were building a powerhouse team around second-year quarterback Jameis Winston. The NFC South was going to be one of the best divisions in the NFL.

The Saints made Dennis Allen their defensive coordinator, who had taken the position on an interim basis following the firing of Rob Ryan, in hopes that the defensive change would take some of the pressure off Brees and the offense.

But the season opener looked to be more of the same old, same old for the Saints as they engaged in a shootout with the Oakland Raiders at home. Brees' third touchdown pass of the game, a 98-yard hookup with Brandin Cooks, provided a 24-10 lead midway through the third quarter, but the Raiders rallied to tie the game at 27 in the fourth quarter. Brees promptly marched the Saints 84 yards on three plays, and his 2-yard scoring toss to Travis Cadet restored a 34-27 advantage.

But the Raiders were not done. Second-year signal-caller Derek Carr engineered an 11-play, 75-yard scoring drive. After Seth Roberts caught a 10-yard TD pass with 47 seconds left, the Raiders made a gutsy decision to go for the win via a two-point conversion, and it paid off when Carr found Michael Crabtree to condemn the Saints to a 35-34 loss.

The loss overshadowed a stellar effort by Brees, who threw for 423 yards and 4 touchdowns without an interception.

The defense showed up in Week 2 against the New York Giants, but Brees and the offense never found a rhythm in their first road game. He had a fourth-quarter touchdown pass to Willie Snead early in the fourth quarter to tie the game at 10 and guided another scoring drive that knotted the game at 13 after Wil Lutz booted a 45-yard field goal with 2:54 remaining. The Giants, though, held the ball the rest of the game and drove 70 yards before Josh Brown kicked a 23-yard field goal as time expired to give New York a 16-13 win.

At 0-2, the Saints were facing a must-win scenario as they hosted the Falcons in a key divisional clash on Monday Night Football to close Week 3. Much like New Orleans, Atlanta possessed a high-octane offense capable of putting up points quickly and in bunches. Both teams came out strong as both Brees and Falcons counterpart Matt Ryan had two first-half TD passes.

But Atlanta enjoyed a 28-17 lead at intermission. The Falcons then took control of the game by taking the second-half kickoff and going 75 yards in 6 plays, capped by a 6-yard scoring run by Tevin Coleman. While Brees finished with 376 yards and 3 touchdown passes, he threw a pick-six on a tipped pass that Deion Jones raced 90 yards with as the Saints lost 45-32 and fell to 0-3. It was the first time in 305 pass attempts dating back to last season that Brees had been intercepted.

Brees had little to show for a fast personal start in which he threw for 1,062 yards and 8 touchdowns while completing 66.4 percent of his passes. The Saints were competing, but they were failing to find that one big play that could get them over the hump and into the win column heading into Week 4 and a game versus San Diego.

It would be the third time Brees would face the Chargers since he left for New Orleans, but this would be the first time he played in San Diego since his departure more than a decade prior. There were plenty of emotions that he needed to work through, and Brees admitted as much to ESPN in the days building up to the game.

"I mean, listen, I've been waiting for the moment to go back there," he said. "I'm trying to make this just like any other game. It's hard to do that, obviously, because it's meaningful. I'm not gonna sit here and tell you that this one may not mean a little bit more. But my preparation remains the same."

Before the game, Brees went to the spot in the end zone where he suffered the shoulder injury that altered his career path and said a little prayer. The prayer was perhaps the most important part of that game for Brees as the Saints came back from a deficit to win the game by only one point. Of course, Drew Brees' passing game was the main factor in that win. Nevertheless, he still downplayed his performance as a collective effort in what was a meaningful win for him and his New Orleans Saints.

Later on, New Orleans traveled to Kansas City hoping to get to the .500 mark for the first time in the 2016 season, but that plan never came to pass as the Chiefs held off the Saints 27-21. Brees had another strong game with 367 yards and 3 TD passes, but he threw another pick-six, with Daniel Sorensen taking it 48 yards to paydirt for Kansas City.

The Saints bounced back to win their next two games to improve to 4-4. Brees threw for 265 yards and a touchdown while adding a rushing score to power a 25-20 win over Seattle. He followed that up with a 323-yard, 3-touchdown effort as New Orleans rolled up a season-high 571 yards of offense in a 41-23 victory at San Francisco. Brees set an NFL record with his 30th game of 300 yards and at least 3 touchdown passes without an interception.

New Orleans had a chance to go over .500, but a difficult obstacle awaited in the form of defending Super Bowl champions, the Denver Broncos. Though the Broncos had moved on at quarterback with rookie Trevor Siemian now under center following the retirement of Peyton Manning, they still had a very capable defense that had forced 16 turnovers, helping them attain a 6-3 record heading into the game at the Superdome.

That formidable Broncos defense caused Brees all sorts of problems but he was still able to able to find his receivers to force the defending Super Bowl champions into a tight battle. However, the Broncos dug deep to beat the Saints with an 84-yard rush that gave them a two-point win.

While Brees lamented to the New Orleans-Times Picayune that "you hate to see a game like that come down to just a simple play," he also took some of the blame for the loss. The Saints had committed four turnovers and put themselves in such a precarious position.

On top of this disheartening loss, the Saints were facing a quick turnaround as they had to face the Panthers on Thursday Night Football, this time in North Carolina. The Panthers were eager for payback from their Week 6 loss and did an excellent job bottling up the Saints' offense.

Brees committed two turnovers that led to 10 points for Carolina, and after Lutz had a field goal blocked, Cam Newton threw a 40-yard touchdown pass to Ted Ginn Jr. to give the Panthers a 20-3 lead with 16 seconds left in the first half. Brees tried to engineer a furious fourth-quarter comeback and threw a pair of touchdown passes, but Carolina held on for a 23-20 win to drop New Orleans to 4-6.

An angry, well-rested Saints team took out their frustrations on the Los Angeles Rams in Week 12, blowing them out 49-21.

Brees threw for 310 yards and 4 touchdowns, with 2 of them coming in the third quarter to create a 21-point lead. New Orleans put an exclamation point on the win with wide receiver Willie Snead throwing a TD pass to Tim Hightower as it racked up 555 yards of offense against one-time Saints defensive coordinator Gregg Williams.

But any momentum gained in that victory was blunted the following week against Detroit. The Lions used a short-passing game to control the ball and keep Brees off the field, and when the Saints did have the ball, they kept Brees out of the end zone. It was the first time in 60 home games he failed to throw a touchdown pass, and the Lions recorded three interceptions in a 28-13 victory.

At 5-7, the Saints were now facing a must-win situation to have any hopes of reaching the postseason. But to a degree, they also held their fate in their own hands with the next two games, the first against division rival Tampa Bay. New Orleans was two games behind the Buccaneers entering its Week 14 showdown in Tampa, but an offense that was so consistently prolific came up short once more.

The Buccaneers had three lengthy scoring drives, but the Saints' defense did well enough to keep them in the game by allowing just a touchdown and two field goals. Brees put together drives around a safety by New Orleans that resulted in a pair of field goals to pull the Saints within 13-8 by intermission. Brees got them within field goal range again to draw within 13-11, but Tampa Bay responded with a field goal of its own to restore the five-point advantage. The fourth quarter encapsulated the frustration of the season for Brees and the Saints; he was intercepted twice trying to direct a potential game-winning drive, and the 16-11 setback all but mathematically ended the team's playoff chances.

Brees took little solace in eclipsing the 4,000-yard mark for the 11th time in as many seasons with the Saints, as the defeat also marked the first time since 2008 he failed to throw a touchdown pass in back-to-back games.

What looked to be an interesting Week 15 game between the Saints and Arizona Cardinals turned into two teams with high-powered offenses playing out the string. Neither disappointed, though, as Brees threw for 389 yards and 4 touchdowns as New Orleans outlasted Arizona 48-41. Two of those scoring tosses went to Cooks, who enjoyed a big day with 7 catches for 186 yards. The win also marked the 21st time Brees had thrown at least four touchdowns without an interception.

Brees and the Saints then gave the Buccaneers a lump of coal on Christmas Eve, avenging their loss in Tampa Bay with a 31-24 victory. Brees threw for 299 yards and a touchdown. Unfortunately, it was not enough to secure a Wild Card spot. Once again there would be no postseason for the Saints.

New Orleans had a chance to finish the season on an up note and with a .500 record at Atlanta, but a motivated Falcons team playing for second in the NFC and a first-round bye in the playoffs proved too much for the Saints. Matt Ryan threw four first-half touchdown passes as the Falcons stormed to a 35-13 halftime lead and then withstood a furious rally by Brees, who had three fourth-quarter TD tosses in a New Orleans' 38-32 defeat.

Despite becoming the first player to reach 5,000 passing yards in a season five times and setting an NFL record with 471 completions, it was a lost season for Brees and the Saints. His quote to the AP after the loss to Atlanta that "I thought we had a better team than what our record ended up being," probably summed up the 2016 campaign best.

While Brees had spoken of the desire to play into his 40s, the other truth was that the window of opportunity to win a second Super Bowl was closing. He was 38 years old and entering the final year of his contract, which also meant the Saints would likely need to evaluate their future at the quarterback position. New Orleans raised some eyebrows in the offseason by trading Cooks to the New England Patriots for a first-round draft pick in the 2017 draft, leading to speculation that a rebuild could be in the future.

For his part, Brees still believed he could create something special for the upcoming season and was determined not to let his contract status undermine that effort.

"I'm trying to put the (contract) conversation to bed just by saying … we can worry about it at the end of the year," he said during a press conference as part of an event for Habitat for Humanity and Marriott in late March. "I think that's what's in the best interest of the team. It's what's in my best interest.

We're so focused on this year, just being in the moment, not thinking about anything beyond this and taking every other year as it comes. But also we're building something here–we are building something. I feel like we have a window of opportunity."

## 2017 Season

Drew Brees, at 38 years old, was already past his prime and was one of the league's elders entering the 2017 season. The good part was that, at the quarterback position, he was not as prone to injuries as other positions were because of the lack of physicality. But the advanced age did not mean that Brees was going to slow down, as he was still planning on playing until he was 40 years or older.

During Week 1 of the 2017 season, Drew Brees finished with a touchdown pass after making 27 completions in a loss to the Minnesota Vikings. Against the New England Patriots and fellow all-time great quarterback Tom Brady in Week 2, Brees once again failed to lead the New Orleans Saints to their first win of the season when he finished with a 60% completion rate. He may have had 2 touchdown passes and 356 yards but it was not enough for him to lead his team to a win.

The New Orleans Saints finally won their first game of the season during Week 3 when they went up against the Carolina Panthers. In what was a statement win, Brees went for 3 touchdown passes, 22 completions, and 220 yards.

A week later, Brees and the Saints kept the Miami Dolphins scoreless throughout an entire game when their defense clicked.

Brees finished that game with 29 completions, 268 yards, and 2 touchdown passes.

The New Orleans Saints managed to win eight straight games after losing their first two outings of the regular season. Even at his advanced age, he was the vital cog that kept the offense running. Drew Brees had a total of 12 touchdown passes and a completion percentage of 73.36% during that entire eight-game winning streak for the Saints.

During Week 13, Drew Brees made history when he was finally able to move up the ladder of all-time great quarterbacks when he passed Peyton Manning for career completions. In that win over the Carolina Panthers, Brees had 25 completions and a single touchdown pass. With that performance, he was second only behind Brett Favre in terms of career completions.

Drew Brees was not yet done in terms of climbing up the ladder of all-time greats.

In the New Orleans Saints' Week 16 win over the Atlanta Falcons, he was able to pass 70,000 career-passing yards and became only the third player in league history to do so. At that time, the only other two players with at least 70,000 passing yards were Peyton Manning and Brett Favre.

Drew Brees finished the 2017 season with 386 completions to lead the entire league in that department yet again. He also led the league in completion percentage with 72%, which was an NFL record at that time. That was the fourth time in his career that he was able to do that and he still proved that he was the league's most accurate quarterback when it came to his passes. He was also ranked the eighth-best player of the 2017 season.

The New Orleans Saints were able to make it as far as the Divisional Round that season after making a return trip to the playoffs for the first time since the 2013 season. However, they lost to the Minnesota Vikings.

## 2018 Season

The truth of the matter was that age had already crept up to Drew Brees as he entered the 2018 season. He was no longer a volume passer who could go over 400 completions in a single season, but the good news was, age only made him smarter and more judicious with his decisions. That was the reason why the New Orleans Saints did not mind giving him a two-year extension worth $50 million.

In only the first game of the regular season, Drew Brees set a record by becoming the all-time leader in the number of 400-yard games as a quarterback. In that loss to the Tampa Bay

Buccaneers, he finished with 37 completions, 439 throwing yards, and a single touchdown.

The New Orleans Saints won their first game of the 2018 season during Week 2 when Brees went for 28 completions and 2 touchdowns. The Saints went on a nine-game winning streak with Drew Brees leading the way with 22 touchdown passes and a 76% completion rate during the entire run.

It was during that run when Drew Brees became the all-time leader in completions. In Week 3, he broke Brett Favre's record when he recorded a total of 6,301 career completions in that win over the Atlanta Falcons. He remained the all-time leader in that department and was far ahead of everyone else except Tom Brady in terms of career completions. The accomplishment only added to his legend and his status as one of the greatest players in the history of the sport. He also earned Offensive Player of the Week honors thanks to that performance.

During Week 5, Drew Brees went on to become the all-time leader in passing yardage when he passed Peyton Manning with 363 yards against Washington. Again, Drew Brees is yet to relinquish his place at the top of the career passing yards ladder.

Against the Baltimore Ravens during Week 7, Drew Brees also became only the fourth player in league history to reach 500 career touchdown passes. He joined Brett Favre, Peyton Manning, and Tom Brady in that department. His legend as an all-time great quarterback was only growing.

Finishing what was once again an amazing season despite his advanced age, Drew Brees led the league in completion percentage after recording a new NFL record of 74.4% in that department. Time only gave him the wisdom to know when to make the right passes and how to become more accurate with his passes, as no other player in the history of the sport was better when it came down to accuracy.

Earning the top seed in the NFC, the New Orleans Saints were the favorites to reach the Super Bowl that season after losing only two games. They defeated the Philadelphia Eagles in the Divisional Round despite a rough start to the game. Brees had 28 completions and 2 touchdown passes in that game to lead his team back to the NFC Championships for the first time in nearly a decade. The last time they made it as far as the NFC Championship Game, they won the Super Bowl.

However, a controversial play during the NFC Championships cost the New Orleans Saints a chance to secure a date with the New England Patriots in what should have been a battle between the two greatest quarterbacks of all time. The Saints lost to the Los Angeles Rams in overtime as a contentious non-call would have helped New Orleans win that game to make it to the Super Bowl.

Despite missing the Super Bowl after spending nearly a decade leading what can only be described as a mediocre team, Drew Brees was able to clearly prove how great of a player he was, even in his later years. He was voted the second-best player in the entire NFL that season and was also second in MVP voting at the age of 39.

## 2019 Season

Playing at the age of 40, Drew Brees had fulfilled his promise of staying in the league for as long as he could. His dedication to staying healthy and fit was what allowed him to play at an elite level even though he was getting older.

In Week 1 of the 2019 season, Drew Brees was able to make 370 passing yards after making 2 touchdown passes and 32 completions. Unfortunately, during Week 2, an injury to his right hand forced Brees to miss all of the Saints' games until Week 8 as he was required to have surgery.

Upon Drew Brees' return in Week 8, he seemed as healthy as ever after making 34 completions, 373 passing yards, and 3 touchdown passes. During Weeks 11 and 12, he once again had three touchdown passes in wins against Tampa Bay and Carolina.

It was during Week 15 of the season when Drew Brees became the all-time leader in career touchdown passes after overtaking Peyton Manning in that department. As such, Brees was solidifying his claim at the top spot in terms of individual talent as a quarterback. He finished the season with 281 completions and a league-leading 74.3% completion rate. Brees also had 27 touchdown passes that season despite missing a lot of games due to injury.

Unfortunately, the games that Drew Brees missed were detrimental for the New Orleans Saints, who had to play a Wild Card game against the Minnesota Vikings. New Orleans ended up losing to the Vikings in overtime as Drew Brees and the Saints bowed out of the playoffs early, just a year after almost making it to the Super Bowl.

Despite playing at the age of 41 at the end of the 2019 season, Drew Brees was still able to secure himself another payday when the Saints decided to keep his services for another couple of years by extending his contract with a $50 million offer.

# Chapter 7: Drew Brees' Personal Life

Make no mistake about it; Drew Christopher Brees is one of the best quarterbacks in the history of the National Football League. However, there is much more to Brees than just his assortment of football records and a Super Bowl ring.

For most people, family comes first, and Drew Brees is no exception. He first met his wife, Brittany Dudchenko, on January 15, 1999, while in college. He recalled seeing her walk across the parking lot toward the apartment complex where he stayed on the Purdue University Campus in West Lafayette, Indiana. Brees was hanging out with several of his buddies to celebrate his 20th birthday, per his 2010 autobiography, *Coming Back Stronger: Unleashing the Hidden Power of Adversity.* He mustered enough courage to approach her. Brees stammered with several cheesy pick-up lines, causing her to shake her head and leave. He remained undaunted, however, convinced that she was the woman he would marry someday.

Brees continued to spot Dudchenko all over the Purdue campus for the next six months. She thought he was nothing but a stalker. For Brees' part, he said he was very confident on the football field. But when it came to meeting women, he was terribly shy.

He crossed paths with her again in the summer. Brees was scheduled to take classes while Dudchenko took on a job. On June 25, 1999, he went with a teammate to a friend's apartment for a party. Brees said in his autobiography he "wasn't a big partier." He was more focused on getting a degree and playing for the Purdue Boilermakers. He saw her walk in with two of her friends, and once they had left her side, he made his move. Dudchenko told him she was about to go back to her apartment to sleep, but Brees knew everyone was going to the apartment complex to swim. She tried to get rid of him in every way possible. Brees even tried to convince her to let him drive her home, but she refused. When he persisted, she relented.

Dudchenko warned Brees that she drove a beat-up 1990 Toyota Celica with a manual transmission. Brees, who had never driven a stick-shift before, shook it off. He had all sorts of trouble driving the car–it took him half an hour to accomplish a five-minute drive. Dudchenko burst out laughing. Nonetheless, Brees invited her to go swimming with his friends and she accepted. They wound up talking for hours in her apartment, discovering that they had a lot in common. It turned out she and her family attended an Episcopal Church. Coincidentally, Brees said he deepened his faith at St. Andrew's Episcopal School in Texas.

"Brittany has certain weaknesses where I have strengths, and I have weaknesses where she is strong," Brees said in his autobiography. "We complete and complement each other."

For example, Dudchenko eats chocolate, has horrible penmanship, and hates math. Brees is quite the opposite–he eats healthy, spells words very well, and computes effortlessly (he was an industrial management major at Purdue). Brees also admitted he does not cook very well while Dudchenko is a master in the kitchen.

They would enjoy many priceless moments together–the 2001 NFL Draft being one of them. She flew in his brother Reid from Colorado for that special occasion. Drew Brees was surprised, to say the least. They all celebrated in his living room as the San Diego Chargers made him the 32nd overall pick that year.

Dudchenko would also be there for Brees during his lowest moments, particularly when he suffered the critical shoulder injury in the Chargers' last regular-season game in 2005. They stayed with her parents in Birmingham while he rehabbed.

Brees proposed to Dudchenko on Valentine's Day 2002 in Paris, France. His rookie season in San Diego had just ended. He planned a European tour without her knowing he would propose to her. He eventually did so at the Le Petit Bofinger restaurant, asking her to marry him in French, and they both cried. A Canadian couple sat to their right. The husband took a photo of the memorable moment and Brees received it in his mail six months later, per his autobiography. Brees and Dudchenko got married a year after they got engaged.

They planned to start having kids in the offseason of 2006, but Brees' injury changed everything. They had to wait for almost three full years before their son Baylen Robert Brees was born in New Orleans on January 15, 2009. The baby weighed seven pounds seven ounces when he came out at 2:22 p.m. It was a double celebration since Drew Brees turned 30 years old that day—the father and son have the same birthday. In his autobiography, he admitted that he and Brittany had just made up the name "Baylen." It was a unique name that they had never heard before.

The Brees family welcomed their second child, Bowen Christopher, on October 20, 2010. "It's official," Brees tweeted (via WAFB.com). "Brit finally gave in. Bowen Christopher Brees. Healthy, happy baby. Big hands, big feet. Brit is great. I am so proud!"[lxxx]

Nearly two years later, the couple celebrated the birth of their third son. Callen Christian Brees was born on August 16, 2012.[lxxxi]

Almost two years afterward on August 25, 2014, they welcomed their first daughter into the world. They named their fourth child Rylen Judith Brees.[lxxxii] She weighed as much as her eldest brother, Baylen Robert, when she was born.

Drew Brees' faith is also important to him. He became a dedicated Christian in high school when he attended First Baptist Church in Austin, Texas with his father, Chip. At the time, he suffered an ACL injury which prompted him to doubt his future as a football player. All it took to resuscitate Brees' dwindling faith was a sermon from Dr. Browning Ware.

In Brees' 2010 autobiography, he said that he was proud to be a Christian.

"I am very proud of my faith," he quipped. "Being a Christian is who I am. I read the Word of God in the Bible every day, and I do my best to live out the teachings found inside. On a daily basis, I ask God to show me his will and allow me to see the purposes he has for my life. I also strive to live with a healthy fear of God."

Brees and his family live by the Biblical verse, "To whom much is given, much will be required." The New Orleans Saints quarterback believes that those who have a lot also have a responsibility to give back to the community and those in need.

With this in mind, he and his wife established The Brees Dream Foundation in 2003. According to the official website, its mission is "improving the quality of life for cancer patients, and providing care, education, and opportunities for children and families in need."[lxxxiii] Drew Brees said his wife's aunt, Judith Zopp, was the main inspiration behind the foundation. She succumbed to lung and brain cancer complications on September 3, 2000. After her death, the couple made it a vow to help cancer patients all over the world.

When Brees signed with the New Orleans Saints in 2006, his foundation also reached out to the victims of Hurricane Katrina and the rebuilding efforts of the city. The Brees Dream Foundation helped restore various infrastructure in the Big Easy, funded childcare programs, and provided teacher salaries whenever necessary. The foundation launched its "Rebuilding Dreams in New Orleans" campaign in June 2007, which involved 12 projects which cost approximately $1.8 million. According to Purdue's official athletics website, Brittany Brees runs the foundation on a full-time basis. It has raised $22 million as of June 2015.[lxxxiv]

The Brees family also supports the Purdue Athletes Life Success Program (PALS), a free camp that uses sports as a platform to teach children about teamwork, discipline, and leadership. Drew Brees and his foundation fund PALS through a charity golf tournament and the Purdue Employers Federal Credit Union, per his autobiography. The Saints' signal-caller is also committed to enhancing Purdue's athletics program. He donated $1 million to the Boilermakers football team on June 19, 2015, per PurdueSports.com.

"We care so much about Purdue University," Brees said. "Purdue has meant so much to me, and it has provided so many things."

Aside from the PALS program, Brees has also touched kids' lives through the Make-A-Wish Foundation. He has met several children, such as Saints fan Devan Muller, over the years. Muller's wish was to attend a Saints practice and mingle with the players. Brees and his teammates fulfilled the wish, taking Muller into their team meeting room and out on the field to play catch football.

Brees has always been into fitness. He had been lifting weights in the gym since high school. In his autobiography, he said he watches what he eats. His dedication resulted in several NFL records and a Super Bowl ring. Thus, it came as no surprise when President Barack Obama named Brees and three-time U.S.

Olympian Dominique Dawes as co-chairpersons of his Council on Fitness, Sports, and Nutrition on June 23, 2010.[lxxxv]

Brees is also a fitness advocate for children. He teamed up with NFL Play 60 in October 2012 to launch "60 Million Minutes Challenge." This program encourages kids to live a fit and active lifestyle and to be active for 60 minutes every day.[lxxxvi]

*Forbes Magazine* ranked Brees 67th in its "World's Highest-Paid Athletes" list in 2015. He earned more than $30 million annually, an average of $20 million from his NFL salary with the New Orleans Saints, and another $11 million in endorsement deals. Among the brands he has endorsed are Wrangler, Nike, PepsiCo, P&G, and Verizon.[lxxxvii]

# Conclusion

Drew Christopher Brees' story is a classic tale of a person who was unsure of where life would take him but found success through faith, dedication, and an unwavering work ethic. Even at an early age, he doubted if he would flourish as a football quarterback. In spite of this, he worked hard, very hard. Who would ever imagine a fourth-string freshman high school quarterback would one day become a nine-time Pro Bowl selection and Super Bowl MVP? It took a lot of guts. Think back to the time Brees used his ACL injury as inspiration to work his tail off in the weight room. It paved the way for successful stints at Westlake High School and Purdue University, and later, for the San Diego Chargers and New Orleans Saints.

Brees also reminded all of us that adversity can strike at any time, even if one were already at the pinnacle of their career. Hard evidence of this was the losing seasons that he had to endure after earning a Super Bowl ring in the 2009 NFL season. Do not forget the heartbreaking playoff losses to the Seattle Seahawks in 2011 and the San Francisco 49ers in 2012. Brees was also shaking off the futility of his last three NFL seasons at that point (the Saints failed to reach the postseason in each campaign). Even in the most difficult moments, Brees found a way to persevere and always looked to the future with hope and determination.

Through it all, Brees has become not only one of the most legendary icons in NFL history but also a person of great generosity and personal achievement. The world is fortunate to have someone like him. He gives back to the community. Brees' selfless attitude has helped restore the city of New Orleans, given hope to cancer patients, and paved the way for the future of children everywhere.

His civic mindedness puts him at the forefront of the NFL when it comes to players who represent their local communities. Whether it's helping one-time teammate Steve Gleason and his fight with ALS or helping rebuild the city of New Orleans from the ravages of Hurricane Katrina, Brees has always been front and center. In some ways, he has grown up with this reborn city now 12 years removed from such a terrible natural disaster.

Drew Brees' commitment to the local community was vocalized following the tragic shooting death of former teammate Will Smith in New Orleans, when he told ESPN.com in April 2016 that "we need to start judging people a little bit more."

"You know, you talk about not being judgmental. But maybe we need to start judging people a little bit more for not taking responsibility for your children. And listen, there's some situations where that just can't be helped ... something tragic happens, and that's a whole other situation. I'm talking about the ones out there that just choose not to have that responsibility."

These are the words of someone who has intimate knowledge, caring, and concern for his community. In a 2015 article for ESPN marking the 10-year anniversary of New Orleans' recovery since Katrina, Wright Thompson recounted how coach Sean Payton took Brees and his wife on what was supposed to be a tour of the finer parts of New Orleans. Instead, it turned into an all-too-real tour of what damage had been done when the coach got lost driving. Houses gutted. Streets flooded. Buildings with orange X's painted on them because they were structurally unsound. It would have been easy for Drew Brees to look away and turn his attention elsewhere. Instead, he and his wife looked within themselves and chose to make a difference in the Crescent City.

One could say that his Christian faith has everything to do with who he is today, and who could argue with that? He proclaimed that he was proud of his beliefs in his autobiography. It has helped him become the man he is and helped him set an example for people from all walks of life, whether you are a New Orleans Saints fan or not.

Playing beyond his 40s, Drew Brees has still persisted thanks to his faith and to his ability to keep himself in top shape despite playing for practically two decades. He is widely regarded as one of the greatest players of all time and he has the numbers and the accuracy to prove it. He has led the NFL in career completions, career completion percentage, career passing yards, and career touchdown passes.

Whatever the future brings, there is no argument about how far Drew Brees has come, from humble beginnings as a second-round pick to someone who has conquered the top of the quarterback leaderboard. He has worked hard to become the most accurate quarterback in NFL history, and his legacy will forever remain to inspire generations to come.

# Final Word/About the Author

I was born and raised in Norwalk, Connecticut. Growing up, I could often be found spending many nights watching basketball, soccer, and football matches with my father in the family living room. I love sports and everything that sports can embody. I believe that sports are one of most genuine forms of competition, heart, and determination. I write my works to learn more about influential athletes in the hopes that from my writing, you the reader can walk away inspired to put in an equal if not greater amount of hard work and perseverance to pursue your goals. If you enjoyed *Drew Brees: The Inspiring Story of One of Football's Most Resilient Quarterbacks,* please leave a review! Also, you can read more of my works on *David Ortiz, Mike Trout, Bryce Harper, Jackie Robinson, Aaron Judge, Odell Beckham Jr., Bill Belichick, Serena Williams, Rafael Nadal, Roger Federer, Novak Djokovic, Richard Sherman, Andrew Luck, Rob Gronkowski, Brett Favre, Calvin Johnson, J.J. Watt, Colin Kaepernick, Aaron Rodgers, Peyton Manning, Tom Brady, Russell Wilson, Odell Beckham Jr., Bill Belichick, Charles Barkley, Trae Young, Gregg Popovich, Pat Riley, John Wooden, Steve Kerr, Brad Stevens, Red Auerbach, Doc Rivers, Erik Spoelstra, Michael Jordan, LeBron James, Kyrie Irving, Klay Thompson, Stephen Curry, Kevin Durant, Russell*

*Westbrook, Anthony Davis, Chris Paul, Blake Griffin, Kobe Bryant, Joakim Noah, Scottie Pippen, Carmelo Anthony, Kevin Love, Grant Hill, Tracy McGrady, Vince Carter, Patrick Ewing, Karl Malone, Tony Parker, Allen Iverson, Hakeem Olajuwon, Reggie Miller, Michael Carter-Williams, John Wall, James Harden, Tim Duncan, Steve Nash, Draymond Green, Kawhi Leonard, Dwyane Wade, Ray Allen, Pau Gasol, Dirk Nowitzki, Jimmy Butler, Paul Pierce, Manu Ginobili, Pete Maravich, Larry Bird, Kyle Lowry, Jason Kidd, David Robinson, LaMarcus Aldridge, Derrick Rose, Paul George, Kevin Garnett, Chris Paul, Marc Gasol, Yao Ming, Al Horford, Amar'e Stoudemire, DeMar DeRozan, Isaiah Thomas, Kemba Walker, Chris Bosh, Andre Drummond, JJ Redick, DeMarcus Cousins, Wilt Chamberlain, Bradley Beal, Rudy Gobert, Aaron Gordon, Kristaps Porzingis, Nikola Vucevic, Andre Iguodala, Devin Booker, John Stockton, Jeremy Lin, Chris Paul, Pascal Siakam, Jayson Tatum, Gordon Hayward, Nikola Jokic, Bill Russell, Victor Oladipo, Luka Doncic, Ben Simmons, Shaquille O'Neal, Joel Embiid, Donovan Mitchell, Damian Lillard* and *Giannis Antetokounmpo* in the Kindle Store. If you love football, check out my website at claytongeoffreys.com to join my exclusive list where I let you know about my latest books and give you lots of goodies.

# Like what you read? Please leave a review!

I write because I love sharing the stories of influential athletes like Drew Brees with fantastic readers like you. My readers inspire me to write more so please do not hesitate to let me know what you thought by leaving a review! If you love books on life, sports, or productivity, check out my website at claytongeoffreys.com to join my exclusive list where I let you know about my latest books. Aside from being the first to hear about my latest releases, you can also download a free copy of *33 Life Lessons: Success Principles, Career Advice & Habits of Successful People*. See you there!

*Clayton*

# References

[i] Morale, Amos III. "Drew Brees Says Reports About the Saints Replacing Him Have 'Absolutely No Validity.'" NOLA.com. 2 December 2014. Web.

[ii] Layden, Tim. "6 Drew Brees: About Face." *Sports Illustrated.* 16 August 1999. Web.

[iii] "Drew Brees Biography." JockBio.com. Web.

[iv] Brees, Drew and Fabry, Chris. "Coming Back Stronger: Unleashing the Hidden Power of Adversity." Carol Stream, Ill: 2010. Print.

[v] "Since Childhood, Drew Brees has Worked on his Throwing Accuracy." *The Associated Press* (via *The Lafayette Journal & Courier*). 7 December 2000. Web.

[vi] "Drew Brees Biography." GaleGroup.com. 1 June 2000 (updated 25 September 2015). Web.

[vii] Bagnato, Andrew. "Recruiters Didn't Want Him Despite his Unbeaten High School Record, and There Were Times When he Didn't Want to Play Football Anymore. But Drew Brees Landed in the Right Place at the Right Time." *The Chicago Tribune.* 7 December 2000. Web.

[viii] Drew Brees Player Profile. PurdueSports.com. Web.

[ix] "1997 All-USA High School Football." USAToday.com. Web.

[x] "Purdue vs. USC Aug. 30, 1998." PurdueSports.com. Web.

[xi] "Purdue vs. Rice Sept. 12, 1998." PurdueSports.com. Web.

[xii] Reinmuth, Gary. "Purdue's Prolific Passer Will Have More Rushing Help This Year." *The Chicago Tribune.* 24 August 1999. Web.

[xiii] Spoor, Mark. "Purdue's Drew Brees Sets NCAA Passing Record in loss at Wisconsin." 10 October 2014. Web.

[xiv] Bill C. "Anatomy of an Upset: The 1998 Alamo Bowl." FootballStudyHall.com. 14 August 2011. Web.

[xv] "Game Summary – January 1, 2000." OutbackBowl.com. 1 January 2000. Web.

[xvi] "Purdue Boilermakers 2000 Preseason Preview." NationalChamps.net. Web.

[xvii] "Ohio State. Vs. Purdue." Winsipedia.com. Web.

[xviii] Moore, David Leon. "Rose Bowl Game Recap." *USA Today Sports*. 2 January 2001. Web.

[xix] Layden, Tim. "Hang Time with his Future up in the Air, Purdue's Drew Brees, Like Many Top Prospects, Lived in a Maddening Limbo from New Year's to Draft Day: Working Out for NFL Teams, Watching his Draft Status Rise and Fall, Never Knowing which Pro Jersey He'd Wear." *Sports Illustrated*. 30 April 2001. Web.

[xx] Kiper, Mel, Jr. "TCU's Tomlinson Wows at Combine." ESPN. 8 March 2001. Web.

[xxi] "2001 NFL Combine Results." NFLCombineResults.com. Web.

[xxii] Thorman, Joel. "Before Chiefs Traded for Trent Green, Drew Brees Thought KC Would Pick Him." ArrowheadPride.com. 23 April 2014. Web.

[xxiii] "Green, Holmes Overpower Sizzling Brees." *The Associated Press* (via ESPN.com). 4 November 2001. Web.

[xxiv] "Drew Brees 2002 NFL Season Game Log." NFL.com. Web.

[xxv] "Brees, Tomlinson Lead Way for Chargers." *The Associated Press* (via ESPN.com). 8 September 2002. Web.

[xxvi] "Drew Brees 2003 NFL Season Game Log." NFL.com. Web.

[xxvii] "Drew Brees 2004 NFL Season Game Log." NFL.com. Web.

[xxviii] "Pennington Leads Winning Drive After Chargers Miss Field Goal." *The Associated Press* (via ESPN.com). 9 January 2005. Web.

[xxix] "Drew Brees 2005 NFL Season Game Log." NFL.com. Web.

[xxx] "Brees, Gates Power Chargers Past Chiefs." *The Associated Press* (via ESPN.com). 30 October 2005. Web.

[xxxi] "Drew Brees 2006 NFL Season Game Log." NFL.com. Web.

[xxxii] "Drew Brees 2007 NFL Season Game Log." NFL.com. Web.

[xxxiii] "Brees' 445 Yards Key Saints' Domination of Jaguars." *The Associated Press* (via ESPN.com). 4 November 2007. Web.

[xxxiv] "Drew Brees 2008 NFL Season Game Log." NFL.com. Web.

[xxxv] "Brees' Big Game Too Much for Bucs to Handle." *The Associated Press* (via ESPN.com). 7 September 2008. Web.

[xxxvi] "Brees Picks Apart Packers' Defense for Four Scores; McAllister Sets Mark." *The Associated Press* (via ESPN.com). 24 November 2008. Web.

[xxxvii] "Mina Brees Died of Drug Overdose." *The Associated Press* (via ESPN.com). 21 November 2009. Web.

xxxviii "Drew Brees 2009 NFL Season Game Log." NFL.com. Web.

xxxix "Brees Overcomes Early Turnovers to Help Saints Stay Perfect." *The Associated Press* (via ESPN.com). 8 November 2009. Web.

xl "New Orleans Saints History." FootballDB.com. Web.

xli "Saints' D Frustrates Brett Favre as Vikings Fall in NFC Title Rematch." ESPN.com. 10 September 2010. Web.

xlii "Drew Brees 2010 NFL Season Game Log." NFL.com. Web.

xliii "Browns Pull Upset of Saints Thanks to Drew Brees' 4 INTs." ESPN. 24 October 2010. Web.

xliv "NFL Standings -2010." ESPN.com. Web.

xlv "Matt Hasselbeck Throws 4 TDs as Seahawks Stun Saints." ESPN. 9 January 2011. Web.

xlvi Evans, Simon. "NFL Announces Lockout of Players." 12 March 2011. *Reuters*. Web.

xlvii Schefter, Adam. "Sources: Deal to End Lockout Reached." ESPN. 25 July 2011. Web.

xlviii Farmer, Sam. "Drew Brees, Aaron Rodgers Can Settle Different Off-Season Approaches, Too." *The Associated Press* (via AL.com). 8 September 2011. Web.

xlix "Drew Brees Sets Single-Season Passing Record as Saints Clinch NFC South." ESPN. 27 December 2011.

l "Drew Brees Throws for 466 Yards, 3 TDs as Saints Pound Lions." ESPN. 8 January 2012. Web.

li "Alex Smith, 49ers Bounce Sloppy Saints, Charge into NFC Title Game." ESPN. 15 January 2012. Web.

lii Vacchiano, Ralph. "New Orleans Saints Coach Sean Payton Suspended 1 Year for Bountygate Scandal; Gregg Williams Out Indefinitely." *New York Daily News*. 21 March 2012. Web.

liii "Drew Brees Signs $100 Million Contract with New Orleans Saints." NFL.com. 15 July 2012. Web.

liv "Drew Brees 2012 NFL Season Game Log." NFL.com. Web.

lv "Saints Back at .500 Mark, Roll Past Raiders for Third Straight Season." ESPN. 18 November 2012. Web.

lvi "Drew Brees Eclipses 5,000-Yard Mark for Record Third Time in Loss." 30 December 2012. ESPN. Web.

lvii Brady, Erik. "The Payton Saint of New Orleans Returns." *USA Today Sports*. 4 September 2013. Web.

lviii "Drew Brees, Saints Hold Off Falcons in Coach Sean Payton's Return." ESPN. 9 September 2013. Web.

lix "Drew Brees 2013 NFL Season Game Log." NFL.com. Web.

lx "Garrett Hartley's Third Field Goal Carries Saints Past 49ers." ESPN. 20 November 2013. Web.

lxi "Drew Brees-Led Saints Reach Playoffs with Trouncing of Bucs." ESPN. 30 December 2013. Web.

lxii "NFL Team Total Defense Statistics – 2013." ESPN. Web.

lxiii "NFL Team Total Offense Statistics – 2013." ESPN. Web.

lxiv "Marshawn Lynch, Seahawks Top Saints to Reach NFC Title Game." ESPN. 12 January 2014. Web.

lxv "Billy Cundiff's Last-Second FG Lifts Browns to Upset of Winless Saints." ESPN. 14 September 2014. Web.

lxvi "NFL Career Pass Completion % Leaders." Pro-Football-Reference.com. Web.

lxvii Terrell, Katherine. "Drew Brees Extends Records in Near-Perfect Game vs. Chicago." NOLA.com. 16 December 2014. Web.

lxviii King, Peter. "An Aging Star, A Lost Season." MMQB.SI.com. 26 January 2015. Web.

lxix "Drew Brees 2014 NFL Season Game Log." NFL.com. Web.

lxx "Quarterbacks Over 35 in the Super Bowl." NBCSports.com. Web.

lxxi "Winston Wins for First Time as Bucs QB, 26-19 Over Saints." ESPN. 21 September 2015. Web.

lxxii Brinson, Will. "Saints QB Drew Brees to Miss Panthers Game with Shoulder Injury." CBS Sports. 25 September 2015. Web.

lxxiii Chase, Chris. "The New Orleans Saints Saved Their Season with Fastest OT Touchdown in NFL History." *USA Today*. 4 October 2015. Web.

lxxiv "Drew Brees Hits 2 Passing Milestones in Saints' OT Win Over Cowboys." ESPN. 5 October 2015. Web.

lxxv Stites, Adam. "Drew Brees, Eli Manning Combine for Most Passing TDs Ever in a Game." SBNation.com. 1 November 2015. Web.

lxxvi "Brees' 7 TDs Help Saints Top Giants, 52-49 on Last-Second FG." ESPN. 2 November 2015. Web.

lxxvii "Texans Top Saints 24-6 for 4th Consecutive Win." ESPN. 29 November 2015. Web.

lxxviii "Stafford Leads Lions Past Saints, 35-27." ESPN. 22 December 2015. Web.

lxxix "Brees Sharp Despite Foot Injury, Saints Beat Jaguars 38-27." ESPN. 27 December 2015. Web.

lxxx Hays, Robb. "New Brees Goes by the Name of Bowen." WAFB.com. 20 October 2010. Web.

lxxxi Tatum, Doug. "Drew, Brittany Brees Announce Birth of Their Third Son, Callen Christian Brees." NOLA.com. 16 August 2012. Web.

lxxxii "Drew Brees Welcomes Daughter Rylen Judith." People.com. 27 August 2014. Web.

lxxxiii Brees Dream Foundation. DrewBrees.com. Web.

lxxxiv "Brees Makes $1M Commitment to Football Program as Master Plan Evolves." PurdueSports.com. 19 June 2015. Web.

lxxxv "First Lady Launches President's Council on Fitness, Sports, and Nutrition." WhiteHouse.gov. 23 June 2010. Web.

lxxxvi "Drew Brees and Kinect Team Up to Combat Childhood Obesity with '60 Million Minutes Challenge.' Gamezone.com. 11 October 2012. Web.

lxxxvii "Drew Brees: The World's Highest-Paid Athletes." Forbes.com. 11 October 2015. Web.

Made in the USA
Columbia, SC
24 November 2020